What people are

Sales S

Rebecca has managed to create a "sales manual" that reveals the sales process in a structured way that is easy to understand and apply. With stories from her own sales career it is both informative and inspiring.

Mike Macedonio, *New York Times* bestselling author of *Truth or Delusion?: Busting Networking's Biggest Myths* and *The World's Best Known Marketing Secret*.

Sales Savvy is a delight to read, laced with entertaining stories it lays out the whole sales process in a simple and digestible structure. Rebecca's mastery in sales shines as she shares her honest account and learnings, providing invaluable insights and tools to help you be more productive with people and in your business.

Leanne Babcock, coach and best-selling author of *Open Me* and *Real & Wild You*

Need to enhance your selling capability? *Sales Savvy* could be what you're looking for. Rebecca's successful 30-year sales career has been forged at the sharp end. Along the way she's created a structure and an approach that works.

Greg Hopkinson, Entrepreneur & founder of 'Animates' retail chain and author of *Boundless*

Sales Savvy

The How-to Sales Handbook

Sales Savvy

The How-to Sales Handbook

Rebecca Parry

BUSINESS
BOOKS

Winchester, UK
Washington, USA

JOHN HUNT PUBLISHING

First published by Business Books, 2022
Business Books is an imprint of John Hunt Publishing Ltd., No. 3 East St., Alresford,
Hampshire SO24 9EE, UK
office@jhpbooks.com
www.johnhuntpublishing.com
www.johnhuntpublishing.com/business-books

For distributor details and how to order please visit the 'Ordering' section on our website.

ISBN: 978 1 78904 816 2
978 1 78904 817 9 (ebook)
Library of Congress Control Number: 2021939172

A CIP catalogue record for this book is available from the British Library.

Design: Stuart Davies

UK: Printed and bound by CPI Group (UK) Ltd, Croydon, CR0 4YY
Printed in North America by CPI GPS partners

We operate a distinctive and ethical publishing philosophy in
all areas of our business, from our global network of authors to
production and worldwide distribution.

Contents

For my daughter Samara

Chapter 1

Introduction

Sales is one of those things where people believe you either have it or you don't. Just like singing, athletic ability or math! And although I do agree in part – there are some attributes that naturally make someone more adept at sales such as their level of social intelligence, confidence and persuasiveness, these are all things that can be developed. Everyone possesses these qualities to some degree and it's about harnessing these in a directed and focused way to be more effective in selling your ideas, products, services or even yourself.

When I started out in sales it was more by accident than by design. Having grown up the seventh child in a family of ten in New Zealand, I was hungry for material success born out of a childhood with much love, but little material means. So, I skipped university in order to get a job and start earning money. After a short stint working at my first job at a bank, it didn't take long for me to realize I was a square peg in the "wrong hole." When I saw an ad in the paper for a sales role where I would earn commission, I was excited. It was a chain of retail stores selling home appliances and it didn't take me long to get my sales bearings. Even then as a young 18 year old woman I recognized the intricacies of the sales process and what I needed to learn. When to pause, ask a question and listen. How to bridge presenting the product to asking the customer if they would like to purchase – and how to do that in a natural way.

Always looking for the next adventure I moved to Australia where I had my first taste of Business to Business sales working for Yellow Pages. As a spritely 20 year old I was telling business owners how they could get a bigger share of business through advertising with the Yellow Pages. From that experience I moved to various sales roles in Australia from selling fax machines to magazine advertising before returning home to New Zealand nine years later. In my early years I was restless and easily bored. I had a short attention span and needed a constant challenge and it wasn't until many years later when I moved to a software development company in New Zealand that I stayed for more than two years – I ended up working for that company for eight years.

In 2018 I moved to the US with an Entertainment Technology start-up to head up their sales drive into the US market. After a very challenging two year period of single handedly trying to break into a tightly controlled US market, we started to see month on month revenue increase and key strategic wins when the pandemic suddenly struck. It was at this time that I put pen to paper and started writing this book.

All told I have worked in over 12 industries in sales roles across three countries and conducted business around the world. Although initially I viewed these changes as a weakness, it has ultimately become my strength. This diversity gives sales depth. Being able to draw on experiences from a wide cross-section of industries instead of following the expected approach in a particular industry has definite advantages. It also encourages creative thinking and adaptability to changing market conditions.

So, if you are like me don't despair. Sometimes your biggest weakness can become your biggest strength. Like many other pursuits where practice makes perfect sales is no different. And importantly life experience counts for a lot. It's just a matter of applying the knowledge and experience you have accumulated over the course of your life in a structured, well-thought-out manner. Sales for all its mystery is actually a very systematic and straightforward process with well-defined steps. In the following chapters I have laid these out for you so that it becomes less magic and more logic injected with your unique self. Because we usually buy the person before we buy *from* the person.

Sales can touch many parts of our lives from selling yourself at an interview, pitching your new business idea to an investor or getting your next consulting project. The purpose of this book is to share some of my sales experience of over 30 years in the hope that it can help propel you on your own path.

You may not be in a sales role, but you might be in a position of influence or leadership or you may be a business leader or entrepreneur. I am writing with **you** in mind and if you also happen to be a seasoned sales professional there will be some nuggets within these pages for you too. Wherever possible I have provided real life examples gathered from working across various industries, countries and sales roles.

Like many of you reading this now, I too have had to adapt to a new world amidst a pandemic that now must accommodate social distancing. Although this changes some aspects of *how* we do business, the sales fundamentals and process remains the same. Where it is relevant, I have added notes on selling in 2020 and beyond and tips based on my own experience in successfully adapting to this new business environment.

At the close of each chapter I have suggested actions/exercises to give an opportunity for practical application of each topic. After all, the purpose of this book is to help you realize your innate sales potential!

So, let's get started.

Chapter 2

Becoming More Influential

Definition of Influence - The capacity to have an effect on the character, development, or behavior of someone or something, or the effect itself.

If I think about the most important factors that build influence which is the cornerstone of sales, I would have to say being confident and likeable. The good thing is that these two qualities can be worked on and developed.

Confidence is a state of mind. So what builds confidence? Action does. Remember your first job and how nervous you were on your first day? Then fast forward one year and you were much more confident doing exactly the same job. The difference? You had performed the tasks in your job many times and as a result built confidence. So how do you appear more confident from the start when inside you might be feeling nervous? Reframing can help. Instead of "I am nervous" say "I am excited." The physical symptoms of nervousness and excitement are exactly the same – the butterflies in your stomach, the sweaty palms, the shallow breathing – but your frame of reference will determine if psychologically you feel excited or nervous and that in turn will affect how other people perceive you.

Once you have decided you are excited your tone of voice will change, your body language will change and even your choice of words and delivery will change to fit with your inner framing of "I am excited." Personally, I notice that whenever I do this mental reframing, I reduce the number of um's and ah's when I am speaking. This small mental shift translates into a significant confidence shift. Try it next time you are feeling nervous and notice the subtle differences. You will be surprised what an impact this can make.

Being comfortable with being uncomfortable

To truly be confident in any situation you will have to start being comfortable with being uncomfortable. Stretching yourself just like stretching yourself physically, will be uncomfortable at first but with repeated application will become easier. This is something I have come to accept. I am naturally a creative "right brain" person and not a natural fit when it comes to technology. In my early sales career, I was drawn to more creative sales roles and industries such as advertising where I was very comfortable. I realized at a certain point in my career that if I wanted to earn to my fullest potential, I had to switch industries and move into technology. This was extremely uncomfortable for me and I even had some early opportunities that I didn't pursue due to my own fear. I turned down an opportunity to work for a web development company when I realized I would have to demo the technology – something that left me in a cold sweat at the very thought of it. Fifteen years on and I was doing just that on my own in a new country in the entertainment industry which I had no experience in. If I hadn't during the previous 15 years become comfortable with being uncomfortable, I would never have been able to make that transition.

It sounds a little cliché, but I would talk to myself on my way to meetings to make sure I was in a good confident space. Did I have nerves? Yes! But I would use the reframing technique from "nervous" to "excitement" and give myself a pep talk as I was navigating Los Angeles' highways – the traffic was almost a bonus as I had more time to mentally prepare.

If you ever find yourself overwhelmed by nerves another technique is to take big deep slow breaths and repeat to yourself "I am relaxed" and visualize yourself being confident and successful in the activity/meeting you are about to undertake. If you observe your breathing when you are nervous it will be shallow and the very act of taking deep breaths tells your nervous system that you are safe and will relax you. Visualization is a powerful technique and one that your subconscious does not differentiate between what is imagined and what is real. Visualizing will both calm your nerves and improve your performance. I used to be a Jazz singer and when I first took to the stage I would be paralyzed by nerves. This technique helped and sales is much like a performance. Once you are relaxed you will naturally be and appear more confident.

Preparation is another key to confidence that is sometimes overlooked. I would rehearse my demos over and over and run through end to end before every meeting. Let's say I had a demo in the afternoon, I would run through it that morning multiple times to make sure I felt confident. I would start right at the beginning with the introduction, so everything felt effortless and natural. Repetition makes perfect and also breeds confidence.

Focus on the other person

Another aspect that can reduce nerves and build confidence is to focus on the other person. For example, if you are about to present think about the person you are meeting and what is most important to them. By focusing on the other person, you will have no room in your thoughts to focus on yourself – which is where nerves begin. What you focus on is extremely important. Thoughts are like a train; they gather momentum and once they gain speed it's hard to stop. Develop a habit to focus on the other person and you will find yourself more relaxed and confident as a result.

The other half of the equation is likeability which confidence enhances. You will become emotionally attractive to people and display the qualities that matter when it comes to how influential you will be. In order to become more likeable there are some attributes that will set you apart.

Be genuine

There is something very special when you meet a person and you feel that you are experiencing their real self. It's much easier to warm to someone who has let go of their protective veneer. We all have them which is why we love it so much when someone drops this and offers their authentic self.

Building rapport and breaking the ice will be much easier and quicker if you can tap into your genuine self. People will instinctively trust you more readily if they feel they are dealing with someone who is being genuine. I recall a survey many years ago now, where people were asked what was the most important quality in a salesperson? Guess what number one was. Being genuine.

Build trust

Trust is so important in being influential. Without trust people won't listen or be led, let alone take on board your ideas or buy from you. Building trust takes time and the currency of trust is "do what you say you will do." If you say you will come back to them in two days with more information, come back to them in two days. If you say you will deliver the proposal in two weeks, deliver it in two weeks. It's not rocket science but it's critical. Even better is to go a step further and under promise and over deliver. If you think it's going to take you a week to complete tell them two weeks and delight them in a week's time and watch their trust in you build.

Under promising and over delivering has been my mantra and I do it automatically. Sometimes it can feel at odds when we are trying to impress but once you over deliver you will truly impress. Of all the different qualities that contribute to being effective in sales doing what you say you will do is probably the most straightforward and will have immediate effect without any reliance on skill or expertise. It's one of those concepts based on common sense that isn't very common.

Have empathy

In order to influence you must understand who you are trying to influence. What are their drivers, what makes them tick and what is important to them? The only way you can understand this is to have empathy and walk in their shoes. It comes in many forms both emotionally, verbally and physically. Once you have empathized emotionally you understand how they feel, you can reflect that back verbally or physically through your body language. When they feel understood they are more likely to be influenced by you.

Empathy also means you can adapt to your audience. Are they more logical? Stick with the facts and say "I think" rather than "I feel." Are they more feeling and emotional? Tell stories and say "I feel" rather than "I think." Are they impatient? Then get to the point. Are they deliberate and slow when they speak? Then slow your own speech. Are they bubbly and more comfortable with small talk? Then be sure to make them feel settled before getting down to business. Empathy means you will mirror the person you are talking to, so you are communicating in a style that they are comfortable with. The more they feel you are like them, the more they are likely to engage with you.

Empathy even helps with problem solving. You need to be able to put yourself in a person's shoes to understand their situation enough before offering a solution. Empathy does come naturally to some more than others, but it's definitely an emotional muscle that can be strengthened. Next time you are having a conversation with someone make it your goal to really understand them. Be an active listener. Listen to what they are saying without thinking about what you are going to say next and repeat back to them your understanding of what they have just said. Ask questions that show you are listening and make the purpose of the question to understand them more. In doing this you will engage with them at a deeper level and build a relationship through empathy.

Connect with people

We have all experienced those moments speaking with someone at a superficial level and no effort is made to truly connect. As soon as we can we want to move on to someone we can better relate to. When we relate to someone on an emotional level, we feel energized and engaged. This is what we need to do if we want to influence – we need to talk to their hearts not their heads. Someone might understand your logic but it's not until they connect with you on an emotional level that they will be propelled to act.

Some of my best sales results have come from dealing with difficult people. I genuinely love to meet new people, which has probably helped not hindered my business development career and I find meeting new people exciting. When I meet someone who at the outset seems a little prickly, I try to find that part of them that is warm and likeable. No one is all bad or all good and if you want to steer someone in a certain direction you need to connect with them first. I almost took this as a challenge with difficult people, spurred on by the fact that my competition was far less likely to engage easily with this person. I also found that as a result of connecting they tended to be very loyal and I was able to build strong long-term relationships that were also hard for the competition to break through.

Positive Contagion

People generally prefer to deal with positive people so having a positive outlook is necessary if you want to increase your likeability. Positivity is on a scale and people tend to sit naturally on some point on that scale. If you are naturally a glass half empty person that's OK, it has its own strength. Some of the most beautiful songs ever written were done so in the depths of despair. Sometimes pessimism can serve. But in sales and being influential it rarely does. So, if you are one of those people you will just need to be a little more conscious of your level of positivity, especially when you are around people. And that goes for those of us who tend to be a glass half full, as we all have our down days. Positivity is contagious and the opposite is true. Just look at how the media can influence our mood through news stories on a daily basis.

Choose to read uplifting material and put yourself in the right mindset before you interact with people. Watch your choice of words, be self-observant and self-correct when you catch yourself phrasing something in a negative tone. Much like exercise being positive becomes a habit and the more you surround yourself with positivity the more you will notice and eliminate the negative. People are attracted to positive people and more often than not repelled by negative people. Be the most uplifting person you can be, and you are on the road to being very influential.

Chapter 3

The Sales Process – Preparation & Research

The sales process is essentially like a funnel where you start at one end with a list of potential customers and by following the steps you reach the end of the sales process with a new customer. These steps can be broadly described as Preparation & Research, Prospecting (the approach), Discovery (understanding their needs and how you can help), Qualification (is this worth your time pursuing), Presentation, Proposal, Handling Objections, Closing, Follow-up and Relationship Management.

The sales process is essentially a framework that applies to any industry. The only difference will be some additional considerations based on the specifics of the business you are in, but the framework and steps in the sales process remain the same. For example, in magazine advertising I will need to understand if the customer is looking for call to action or branding advertising and this in turn will help me understand the solution and also any potential competitors such as radio, online advertising or sponsorship. Alternatively, in software development I will need to understand my customer's preference between bespoke development, an "off the shelf" product or a SaaS model which will feed into the qualification process, the solution and who my competitors might be. With both examples the steps remain the same but some of the finer details and considerations will change within the framework. Over the following chapters I'll walk you through each step in the process and provide details and hints and tips on each step.

Preparation & Research

There are a number of areas that you will need to research and prepare before you make an initial approach and I will go through each with you.

Understand your offering and point of difference – this is possibly the most important part of your sales preparation. Understanding what sets you apart from your competition. With changing jobs so frequently, I found myself doing this a lot and it was my first priority as I was getting my bearings in a new sales role. Sometimes this can be difficult especially if you are in a "vanilla" industry with few differentiators. When I moved to corporate travel there was very little difference between companies who were all vying for the same customers. Often the key differentiator was the service an individual travel consultant could offer but all corporate travel agents could say the same thing. I kept digging and discovered that our online travel booking system was not used by any of our competition and using the tool saved customers money as they were able to compare fares and reduce booking fees. It also addressed the key reason someone would change corporate travel agents – to save money. If you look hard enough you will find something that sets you apart.

Understand your market – what companies need your product or service and what part of the market are they in? Do you have a sweet spot where your offering best meets the needs of that part of the market? For example, when I worked for a small Graphic Design and Web development company, I realized early on our key differentiator was we could offer the quality of services demanded from a large corporate but at a fraction of the cost due to our size. I targeted what we call in New Zealand, Non-Government Organizations or NGO's who needed the same service as the large corporates but had smaller budgets.

The NGO's gave us credibility and profile, becoming the steppingstone to bigger account wins and the business started to grow.

Understand the decision-makers and influencers – What type of person or role would you need to engage with to sell your product or service? Are the decision-makers at the executive level with managerial level influencers and who are they and what do they do? Identifying who they are means you can tailor your approach to the individual and what would drive them. Once you have identified your market, customers and contacts, start building a list from the resources available to you. This could be industry publications, Industry associations, LinkedIn, referrals and networking. The aim is to have a solid list from which you can start prospecting.

Know the competition – understand how your offering differs from your competition both strengths and weaknesses. At the start, your understanding may be limited but as you prospect and meet with potential customers you will develop an inventory of knowledge of your competitors. My recommendation is to focus on your own game at first and don't get too bogged down with knowing what your competition is up to. As you pick up competitor information take note and use it where you can, but in a positive slant and without naming them. For example, if you discover a weakness in the competition highlight the area where your product or service addresses this weakness. If the client is familiar with the competitor, they will take note.

As your sales pipeline and number of customers develops you may want to consider a more formal SWOT Analysis – Strengths, Weaknesses, Opportunities & Threats. It's sometimes a good way of understanding from a strategic point of view the health of your business and this can inform your sales strategy. Alternatively, you can apply this approach to an individual customer to understand the best sales strategy to take to maximize the opportunity.

Know your product – before you can effectively sell you need to have a solid understanding of your offering. Think of the different scenarios/use cases or customer problems and how your offering solves these problems so that opportunities can be identified in the Discovery phase. Your customers are also trying to understand the market and what is out there as part of their evaluation and buying process. If you can help them due to your thorough product knowledge, you will become a trusted confidante – the ideal position to be in when selling.

Be sold on what you are selling – if you're not sold no one else will be. You really need to truly believe that what you have is something that has true if not exceptional value. How you feel about what you are selling will come across and determine very quickly how successful you will be. If you are not sold, you will either need to discover through the steps I have outlined above what your value proposition is or don't proceed. This is essentially a self-qualification step. To give you a great example of how important this is, when I started with the Yellow Pages in Australia I was given six weeks sales training. At the end of the training they took us out on the street to interview people at random. We were to ask them if they had used the Yellow Pages in the last month. Every person I spoke to had, which was the case with everyone else in the class too. Not only that but most of them had used the Yellow Pages in the last week! That day we were all sold and became evangelists – in our sales trainer's words "we were bleeding yellow."

Exercise
I recommend you buy a journal or exercise book for notes to complete the exercises throughout this book. For this exercise write a list of

all of the unique selling points or key differentiators you believe you have. Is there one that stands out that is truly unique? Take note as this is what we will use to develop your approach.

Chapter 4

The Sales Process – Prospecting & the Approach

How you approach a potential prospect can depend on a few things. Who are they and how do you know them? Is this a "cold" or "warm" prospect as in, do they know who you are and do you have an existing relationship? It's best to take an approach that you are comfortable with especially if you are new to prospecting. There really is no right or wrong way it's a matter of working with what works for you and what will be more effective for the type of person you are approaching. I've highlighted the various methods below and tips on each:

Phone

Twenty years ago, before the proliferation of email this was the primary method of contacting someone. Over the years this has changed to such a degree that now Millennials are somewhat uncomfortable with communicating via the phone. Despite these changes, other than meeting in person, the phone is probably the most personal way to communicate. With every phone call you are also building a relationship, much more so than over email.

For prospecting in particular, you will want to have a rough script that you feel comfortable with. You will have a few minutes at most to capture their attention and this is best done with a rehearsed script that highlights your point of difference in a succinct and engaging way. At the start of the call I will often start with "the reason for my call" as this will help silence the question in their head and make them more likely to listen to what you are going to say next. How you end your phone pitch is also important. I often end with an "assumptive close" asking them what date they would like to meet. I have had some people set up a date right there and then! The downside is that I don't get a lot of information to help prepare for the meeting, but the plus is I got the meeting! This is quite bold, and you will have to feel comfortable with it.

What will most likely happen is they will ask questions. And really this is the best thing that can happen. Now you have an opportunity to engage and find out more. Ultimately the purpose of the phone call is to see if they have a need that is great enough for them to ideally meet with you or at least progress to a next step. Another way to direct the conversation is to answer a question with a question. Be careful with this or it will come across as avoidance, but if you use it with a soft enquiring tone you will quickly drill down to the information you need to see if there is an opportunity here to progress. With your questions be sure to ask open ended questions where possible – what, where and who (avoid **why** it's a very strong word and can be off-putting, replace with "what was the reason" which is much softer and comes across less aggressive or confronting). The open questions will prevent a simple Yes/ No response which will stop you in your tracks. Try it now. Ask yourself any question starting with what, where or who and try answer with a yes or no answer – you can't. Information is the lifeblood of sales and you want as much as you can possibly get to qualify and progress the opportunity.

Phone manner – without visual cues your voice is the only way a person at the other end of the phone can gauge if they like you and want to deal with you. That means you will need to be extra conscious of your vocal tone and how you are coming across on the phone as they will hear your emotions. You might even want to record yourself first to check how you sound. If you sound flat, try to add more bounce into your voice – an old trick is to smile as you talk, and this comes through in your voice. Even better if you can find something that makes you laugh; this will put you in a positive mood and you won't need to fake it! We all have down days from time to time and if you are planning to make calls on a bad day – don't. You will be wasting your prospect opportunities. If for some reason I'm having a bad day I won't make calls as it's hard to mask and I'll be less effective over the phone. Move to email until you are back to your best self again!

Gate Keepers – If you are calling someone who is senior you will likely encounter a gatekeeper. The best way to handle gatekeepers is treat them like you are talking with the actual person – they are going to decide whether to put you through based on their perception of you. Be warm and courteous and ask for the person by first name only which sounds more familiar. I will often send an email first followed by a phone call so I can say I am calling about the email if they ask what it is regarding. If they press further, you will have to have a succinct pitch that might get you through. I got a clever tip from a boss which is to try different phone numbers based on someone else's direct phone number to see if you get through directly to the person. If you get someone else, you can say "Oh I was trying to get through to such and such but must have the wrong number" and they will often put you through! There is no full proof way of getting past a gate keeper but with trial and error and some persistence your odds will increase.

Email

Sometimes the only way you will get through to someone is by email. With emails make sure your language is professional, to the point but also warm. You will need to have a "hook" and a call to action. The hook is your unique selling point and it should be in the subject line. The call to action should come at the close of the email and will be inviting them to the next step.

Where you can, personalize the content to the receiver and the type of person and role they have. The more it feels like you are sending an individual email specifically to them and less like it is part of an email blast the more likely they will respond. As I mentioned earlier, I will often email first and then call. The benefit of this is that if you get through to the person you can mention that you are following up regarding the email and it makes them more likely to engage.

Mail

Yes, in this age of high tech there is even a place for "snail mail." The novelty factor works well here since most people very rarely receive mail these days unless it's a bill. Handwriting an envelope with a stamp so it appears personal makes it much more likely it will be opened. You will want to have something compelling inside based on your USP and ideally with an introductory letter that is hand signed. Like the email, the letter should have a hook and call to action at the end. I used this method very successfully when I arrived in Los Angeles with my entertainment technology company. I had virtually no relationships in Hollywood so had to start from scratch. We decided to create a beautiful brochure that highlighted a part of our technology that no one else could offer. I added a letter that summarized this with the call to action being a demo. I can't tell you how many letters I signed, envelopes I wrote, and stamps I licked but it was all worth the effort. My approach was to wait one - two weeks after I had mailed them out to call. I got meetings with some very senior studio executives that I otherwise wouldn't have got, especially given we had a very low profile in the market when I first arrived.

About a year after I first arrived in Los Angeles, I was reading the entertainment news which I do most days as it's a rich source of leads. I read an article about a new production company, so I did some research on the company and found the name and contact details of their Head of Physical Production – a key decision maker for the type of technology we offered. I sent him a brochure and letter just as I described earlier and a week after sending it out, I received a call. It was their VP of Physical Production who reported to the Head of Physical Production and he was very excited about our technology. From the phone call I booked a meeting and presented to the key people including their CTO and the Head of Physical Production. The meeting went well, I sent a proposal and we had a subsequent meeting where we discussed costs and we shook hands (literally) on a deal. As I write this, the movie is about to be released in theaters *Unhinged* starring Russell Crowe (a fellow New Zealander who was also amazed by our technology on set!) and after the shoot we developed a case study that has been very useful in articulating our USP to prospective customers. This all came from a little bit of research, sending a handwritten brochure to get their attention and following the steps of the sales process that I will share with you in the following pages.

In person

In some industries there is a geographical element with assigned "territories" that a salesperson will cover. When the salesperson has meetings, it presents an opportunity to do a cold call whilst they are in the area. I did this when I was selling fax machines for Pitney Bowes in Melbourne Australia – yes it was the 90's when they were still widely used! My territory was the Central Business District CBD or what is more commonly referred to as Downtown in the States. We had a term "sandwich calls" which meant going to the businesses either side of the business where you had the meeting. The idea behind it was that by saying you had just met with customer X whom they would most likely know since they were neighbors, they were more likely to engage. It was a useful way of creating more leads and making sure the territory was covered. It's certainly not for the faint hearted as it's a bold thing to do, physically knock on a door to make an unsolicited sales call, but it's worth mentioning here as another way to build a sales funnel with leads.

Referrals

Referrals are of course the best way to introduce you to a new customer and if it can be an introduction from a third person even better. Always get back to the referrer to say thank you after you have progressed with the new customer. Showing appreciation and saying thank you is important and sometimes just this one small action will set you apart – and may bring you more referrals. Professional social media sites such as LinkedIn can be another way of connecting and staying in touch. Especially as people move to new companies it can open up a new opportunity for you. And because it's outside of company email people may be willing to share more with you.

Networking

A quick note on networking events which are a great way of meeting new people or building stronger relationships with people you know. Sometimes these can feel a little daunting especially if you don't know anyone. In that case when you arrive seek out the host. He or she may be with a group or individual and might introduce you which breaks the ice for you immediately. Otherwise ask the host if there is anyone they would suggest you meet and would they introduce you. I think "breaking the circle" is probably the most difficult moment and some people find it easier than others. Observe the room and pick a group that looks less intensely in a conversation so that it's easier to break into their conversation. Go in and confidently say "Hi" and introduce yourself. Some of the conversation starters can be "how do you know the host or company" or if it's an event with a particular topic or product launch you can ask for their thoughts, or you could take a more general approach "what's happening in your business/industry that's exciting/ interesting at the moment?" The one question to avoid is "what do you do?" as it creates a negative feeling and best to avoid it early on, although once you are positively engaged with the person it's usually fine, but I do generally tread very carefully with that question. And don't forget to bring plenty of business cards! After the event always follow-up with the people you meet with a thank you email and connect on LinkedIn. This is essentially a lead which is now part of your sales funnel.

Notes on 2020 and beyond

Now that we are in a world where people are primarily working from home some of the approaches above may not work as well, if at all such as in person. For example, mail going to a company address may not find its way to someone's home address where they are now working remotely. However, if you have the person's phone and/or email address this approach can still work for you even in today's climate. On many occasions when I called someone one-two weeks after sending out the printed brochure, they had in fact not received it and if I didn't already have their email address, it was often given freely in order to send a digital copy. The fact they didn't receive the printed brochure didn't negatively affect the results in the end. The same will be true today.

Exercise

Write a phone script and practice so that it feels natural and flows. If possible, practice with another person and make sure you cannot see each other so that you are replicating the experience on the phone without visual cues. Try to ask open questions if possible. Get feedback from the person and if you can't roleplay with someone, record yourself so you can hear your voice and practice. Remember to smile and see if you can hear the difference.

Chapter 5

The Sales Process – Discovery

Now that you have developed a pipeline of leads it's time to develop these into genuine qualified opportunities. The Discovery phase is all about understanding the customer and their needs, before confirming there is a fit for your offering. This is where your creative brain can help. Sometimes it's not obvious at first if there is a good fit, but by asking the right questions and exploring in more depth you will discover if there is an area where you can help. And helping is where it starts and ends. The Discovery phase is where you start to build the relationship and if you do this with the mindset of trying to help, you will get more buy-in from the customer and build trust which is the foundation of any business relationship. You will also find that they will be more forthcoming with information that is going to help you in this process.

The purpose of the Discovery phase is to have a solid understanding of the customer and their business, what their needs are in order of priority, how you can meet these needs and how they will make their buying decision and timeframes. Ticking off all of these is part of the process of qualifying the opportunity and if you can't tick these off you have further work to do to complete this phase.

The Meeting

Although, there are some opportunities that can be progressed and closed over the phone (my first business to business sales role was 100% telephone sales) for most opportunities you will probably achieve a lot more and faster through a face to face meeting. Let's assume for the purposes of learning that you have set a face to face meeting.

This first meeting is of utmost importance as it will set the tone for future meetings, set expectations and create long lasting first impressions that can be difficult to shift. It can quite literally set you up for success or failure. Let's look at some key factors that will help you succeed.

What you wear

Human beings are social animals and it's part of our survival mechanism and biological evolution to fit in. We are hardwired to find common ground and search for common connections. This is to help us determine whether we like and trust this person we have just met. One of the first things we will notice about someone before we even shake their hands or utter a word is what they are wearing and we make all kinds of assumptions about that person from how they present themselves. As a result, it's important we help establish positive first impressions through how we present ourselves. To help this it's important to dress to a similar level of formality or informality to help establish the perceived common ground and put the person at ease. For myself personally having worked across very different industries with a big variation on expected business attire, I have learnt this lesson only too well.

On one occasion after I had moved from IT Recruitment to Radio advertising, I had a meeting with a customer, the owner of a menswear retail shop for the first time. I happened to be wearing that day one of my favorite outfits that was a little more formal but very modern. I felt confident and I had been paid compliments on that outfit many times. When I walked into the shop I asked for the owner and he came out from the back of the store. I introduced myself, shook hands and he quickly took me out back to show me the problem – he had been burgled overnight. I quickly realized that he had mistaken me for the insurance assessor who was expected that morning. This incident made me re-evaluate how I dressed. What I have found is that I need to adjust to suit the level of formality or informality of the industry. That has meant my work wardrobe has changed significantly over the years! After radio I moved into more corporate roles for over 10 years before moving to Hollywood which is much more relaxed. Each time I've had to readjust what I wear to set the right first impression.

One thing to note here for women in particular, is that I have found it's better to be slightly more formal than who you are meeting. In some industries especially ones that are male dominated, there is still some unconscious bias towards women. This means it's going to take a little bit longer for women to establish credibility but don't let that deter you. First impressions are just that and what matters most is how you are perceived over the longer term. However, you might as well stack the odds with you not against you and present yourself professionally, matching the attire of the people you are meeting and lifting the formality up just a notch is a great place to start.

Body Language

Body language is a big topic and could be a book on its own – such as from body language expert Alan Pease. So, although I won't go into any great depth here, I will cover some key elements as it relates to sales.

Positive body language projects a lot about who you are and can set the tone of a meeting. When we are nervous, our body language reflects our inner emotional state and tells the world how we are feeling. To counteract this, try to become more conscious of your own body language and change it to a more confident stance. For example, be aware of your shoulders and pull them back and stand straight with your feet confidently planted on the floor. Keep your posture open and towards the person you are speaking to with direct eye contact – this communicates confidence. As I walk into an elevator to a meeting, I start this process and become more conscious of my body language. That way you are set even before you get to the reception desk.

When you greet the person you are meeting, be sure to look them straight in the eye with a broad smile that includes your eyes. Everyone can detect a false smile that is from the mouth only and doesn't include your eyes. A real smile will put the person at ease, and they will warm to you much more quickly.

Once you are seated and the meeting has begun, notice the other person's body language. If it's a meeting with multiple people you will need to scan the room to pick up body language cues whilst talking with an open posture and with direct eye contact towards your audience. You will notice if they are engaged, they will start to lean forward with an open stance. If you find this doesn't happen take note. Is it across the board or specific people in the room? Are they distracted e.g. with their phones or are they just not engaging? You need to understand what their state is and adjust your pitch accordingly.

The other thing you can do is what's called mirroring. Have you ever noticed when you are talking with someone you really enjoy being with, such as a friend, that you often mirror each other's body language? If your friend is holding their head in their hands so are you. If they cross their legs, you find yourself doing the same. If you ever see this happen in a business meeting you know that you are engaging positively with that person. What I have done at times to help this process is to mirror my body language with the person I am talking with. You can do this in a subtle way to help build engagement and rapport. Try it next time and watch what happens and notice if this helps.

Another part of body language that is ubiquitous and where strong first impressions are made is the handshake. There are a few points to a good handshake. As previously mentioned, look them in the eye with a smile as you shake hands and introduce yourself. In the case where you are waiting at reception and they approach you make sure your right hand is free from bags, keys etc and stand up to shake hands. The handshake needs to be "Goldilocks just right" not too firm like the "bone crusher" and not too soft like the "limp fish." For women especially it's important to have a firm handshake to be perceived as confident and assertive. Practice with someone and get their feedback to make sure you're getting it right.

Another note for women here, is sometimes after you have built a strong relationship both men and women can be less inclined to shake hands, and this is OK. In fact, it can be a great sign! It's just that it's not the social norm for women to shake hands and once the initial meeting and shaking of hands has been established, they may be more comfortable with a hug, a kiss on the cheek or nothing at all – especially women meeting with women. This is absolutely fine if it's not the first time you are meeting, and I will often wait for the person to hold out their hand before I reciprocate. The main thing here is putting the person at ease and matching their preferences and body language. On the other hand, if it is a first meeting, I will always put out my hand to establish a strong first impression and credibility. It doesn't happen often, but occasionally as a woman you may meet an older man who doesn't put out his hand. As a woman it's extremely important in this situation that you do, to set the right tone and establish an equal footing.

Small Talk

Small talk is all about making someone feel comfortable and establishing common ground. At the first meeting there will be moments where you will need to do this. For example, after the first handshake and greeting when you are walking from reception to the meeting room. When you first sit down to talk and before you start talking "business." At the completion of the meeting either in the room or walking back to the elevators. In all of these scenarios there is nothing worse than an awkward silence and this is where the ability to have small talk will make everyone feel more comfortable. This is another one of those "practice makes perfect" skills and the more you do it the more it will come naturally. I often use visual cues as topics. Wherever you are look around you and note what is interesting. Is there a picture or art on the wall? Is there a beautiful view out the window? Do they have something specific to their industry on display? Do they have books on display – this will show what they are interested in. Use this as conversation starters. If you are walking through the building to the meeting room observe anything of interest or unique to the setting and comment on it.

What I will typically do is make a statement that invites a response. For example, "that's an amazing view you have from your office how do you manage not to get distracted?" or "I loved the video you have playing in reception who produced it?" and so on. You will find there is a huge source of inspiration for small talk in your immediate environment and you will quickly put the person at ease and establish rapport. Alternatively, you can use the information gleaned from your research on the company and the person you are meeting, to provide conversation starters. Who are they following on their LinkedIn profile and do you have common connections for example? From your research you will discover aspects that can become conversation topics. Sometimes through small talk you will even get priceless information that you wouldn't have otherwise gotten!

Structure of the meeting

The purpose of the meeting is as I described at the start of this chapter is to have a clear idea by the end of the meeting the type of opportunity and if it is worth progressing, the best way to do so. In order to establish this, you need to follow a basic structure to the meeting to get out of it all that you need.

Introduction – after you are seated and finished with the initial small talk and formal introductions (if it's a group meeting) you will need to introduce your company and offering. As a side note if you are in a group meeting and doing formal introductions be sure to copy their level of intro. For example, if they give name only do the same, if they give name and role or name, role and purpose of role do the same. Wherever possible mirror your actions and approach to the client. An effective company introduction will be succinct and not too long and will give them an understanding of where you fit in the market and what is unique about your offering. Include in this brief introduction some background to the company and/or personal history to help set the scene.

Ask about their problem or what they need – Start the meeting with asking them what they need first and this will help you shape the discussion and keep it relevant to the customer. Remember to ask an open question here to get the conversation started. For example, "Tell me about what you are looking for and what problems you are experiencing currently" something along these lines that is consistent with your personality style is a great way to start.

Ask questions – asking questions is not so much a step but a process throughout the meeting. However, it is best to ask early in the meeting so you can tailor the conversation and/ or presentation to what you have discovered. Be sure to ask the question and be quiet to give the person plenty of room to answer and never for any reason interrupt. Also, try to make it conversational and ask open questions wherever possible. Be an active listener and use your body language to show you understand such as nodding, smiles etc. Summarizing your understanding of what they have just said is another way of showing you are listening and understand. Don't be afraid of asking some more direct questions such as "what is your budget" and when you ask this wait for their answer even if it means a few seconds of silence while they gather their thoughts. The worst they can say is "I'm not in a position to tell you" and at best they will tell you their budget which is valuable information. If you apply the principles of being influential – being confident and likeable to build trust this will help you with your questioning skills. Over time with practice you will become more proficient and build trust early which will allow you to illicit information in a way that makes people feel safe to share with you.

Present your offering – Once you understand what they need and how your offering can help, you then need to present back to them how you can meet their needs. Personalize this so that every description of your product or service is explained in the context of the customer's situation and needs. When you present make sure you pause from time to time to allow them to ask questions and ensure what you are saying is relevant. Continue to observe the room and look for body language to confirm that you are engaging with them. If not, you will need to change tack. I always feel more comfortable when there is a lot of input and discussion with the customer rather than me talking most of the time. If I ever find myself in that situation, I take stock, and look to ask a question in order to put more balance in the interaction. People love to talk about themselves and their situation and a sales situation is no different.

Summary of your understanding and next steps – once you have come to a natural conclusion of presenting and asking questions and you feel you have all you need, it's time to summarize your understanding and confirm next steps. Whatever you do don't walk out of the room without an agreement on what will happen next. This should happen with every step of the sales process – an agreement on the next step. Even a phone call at the early contact stage or at follow-up stage should always end with what you will do next and when.

My final note on the meeting is to come prepared for anything. Whatever you are expecting to happen at the meeting plan and be prepared for all possibilities. As part of preparing for the meeting you may confirm who will be there and what they want you to cover, however this may change and not be communicated with you. Coming from New Zealand where the business culture is to give detailed feedback and information, I got caught out early on. I had to adapt to the US culture where not as much feedback or information is provided and the onus is on you to be prepared for anything. Having experienced this, I think it's a great idea whatever the predominant business culture is or where you are doing business. Things change so be prepared.

Notes on 2020 and beyond

For the time being, meetings will be video meetings which changes the dynamic significantly. Video can tend to dampen down how you come across including warmth and vocal tones in a similar manner as the phone does which I cover in chapter 13. Remember to smile, talk a little more slowly, and pause frequently to give others the opportunity to speak and ask questions. Give consideration to your video set-up, you should have good lighting, try to have the screen lifted up so you are looking squarely at the screen and not down. Your backdrop should be clean and uncluttered and not distracting – and some video platforms have the option of adopting a virtual background. Make sure that you are not in front of light filled windows that can become very distracting when the light changes as you move slightly. You can always run a "Zoom Test" to make sure you are projecting the right video image. Become familiar with the different video platforms so if you have to share screens, chat or invite someone you know how to do this smoothly. And don't forget to turn off your notifications and remove any documents on your desktop and out of sight if you do have to share the screen. Remember everyone else is in the same position. In fact, I had video meetings before the lockdown with Hollywood executives who found it to be more time efficient and these opportunities progressed in the same way as face to face meetings did. Don't let the fact you can't meet with them personally deter you as it's not entirely new.

The other dynamic that may change for the longer term is the business handshake. It will be interesting to see if this fully returns. Personally, I think that it will, but it will be socially acceptable to *not* shake hands. When the world reopens and we find ourselves in physical meetings once again, my advice would be to follow what the person wants to do and reciprocate. If they put out their hand follow suit, but if they don't let it be – it's likely that after everything that's happened, they are no longer comfortable with shaking hands. In fact, one of my last meetings before the lockdown in Los Angeles in March was with a Producer and Post Supervisor. One was happy to hug and the other politely refused to shake hands – we did a "Footshake" instead.

Exercise

Role playing is really helpful to develop your pitch and to get familiar with the right questions to ask for your industry and offering. If you can do this with someone else to get feedback that is great, but if you can't practice your introduction, list the important questions you will need to ask and practice presenting. Again, practice makes perfect!

Chapter 6

The Sales Process – Qualification

Qualifying an opportunity means that it is worth spending your time on and likely to result in a sale. I have put qualification at this point in the process since after you have had the first meeting you have reached a milestone with most likely new information that you will use to *requalify* the opportunity. The qualification process starts in preparation and for some opportunities you will qualify out after research. If from your research, it looks like they have a need that you can fill, after the first contact via phone or email you will have the next opportunity to continue to qualify. And on it goes. At each stage of the sales process you continue to qualify. There are two reasons for this. One is that you want to clearly understand their needs and that your solution fits their requirements and that there is sufficient budget, time and motivation on their part to make a purchasing decision. The other part is to understand enough to counter any competition or change in their buying process to stack the odds in your favor that they will purchase from you and not your competition.

Let's take a look at the different aspects of qualifying an opportunity:

The need – probably the most important is understanding what their needs are in enough detail so that you are confident that your solution meets their requirements. Ultimately a customer is purchasing to solve a problem or take advantage of an opportunity. Your offering has to solve the problem they have or give them a competitive advantage in their own business – if this is a "BTB" business to business sale. If it's not BTB the same principles apply – the person has a problem that needs to be solved or they want to take advantage of an opportunity. For example, let's say you are selling gym memberships. A person comes into the gym who is not currently with a gym and has been told by their doctor they need to start exercising in order to avoid a heart attack. Another prospect belongs to a gym that is a 10 minute car ride away when she walked past your gym on her way to her morning coffee. She wants the convenience of walking to her local gym without the need for parking. The first example is a problem that needs to be solved, the second presents an opportunity for the buyer.

The timeframe – now that you know they have a need that you can fill, timing is important. Understanding when they need the product or service in place and how long their decision-making process will take.

Decision-making process – understanding exactly how they will make their decision and who will be involved. This could be any number of informal or formal processes. The most informal and straightforward would be dealing with a single decisionmaker with no other person involved. Even then, they could be influenced by other people in that decision-making process, so understanding who the influencers are as well as the decisionmaker/s is also key. At the other end of the scale you have the more complex buying process that could even include multiple companies and a formal evaluation process such as an RFI (Request for Information) or RFP (Request for Proposal). These generally include a written response to a client's RFI/P document and a formal presentation but not necessarily both. The best way to get the details you need is to simply ask "what is your decision-making process?" and you will usually get what you need from that one question.

Their Budget – knowing what their budget is will qualify them in or out, or provide the opportunity to tailor your offering to fit to their budget, if that is possible. A lot of people are afraid to ask this question but if you have built rapport and trust there is no reason not to ask. The worst is they won't tell you, but you will be surprised how many times you will get an answer to this question. Just be sure to ask and wait for a response. If they take a minute, it's sometimes because they are thinking through if they can give you the information or how much they can tell you. After you have asked don't start to talk and take them off the hook with a response to your question. I discuss this further in chapter 10 in Closing & Negotiating. It's important when you ask a question like this to wait for a response. If you don't, the conversation will move on and the opportunity to qualify the opportunity on budget will be lost.

Who else are they talking to? – at the end of the meeting I will often ask "Who else are you talking to?" and I will usually get a list of names. I now know who my competition is. If they can't give me that information – sometimes due to a more formal procurement process – I will sometimes get at least *how many* companies they are talking to which is also useful information. As with point number 4 this is the type of question where you need to give them room to respond and be silent while you wait for an answer.

What effort will it take to pursue or respond to the opportunity? – this is probably the last question to answer as the effort required should be in direct correlation with the value of the opportunity and the likelihood of winning. For example, in Professional Services if you need a highly skilled person to help with the response or proposal this same person is no longer available to charge per hour for the time they are required to help with the bid. This is an opportunity cost that needs to be factored into your qualification process. And even if you are not in the Professional Services industry there is still time and energy required to manage the sales process. Let's say you have an opportunity with many competitors, you do not have a strong USP, the company is primarily making a decision based on cost, and the response requires a significant amount of time and effort – these combined factors would qualify it out.

Industry specific qualifications

Often there will be industry specific information you will need to get in order to properly qualify an opportunity. Every industry has its own unique market and competition within it that will determine what this additional information might be. For example, when I was working in software development, I was working with a company that was a Gold Microsoft Partner that had made a strategic business decision to work exclusively with Microsoft technologies. That meant for me I had to also qualify based on the customers likelihood to go with Microsoft as opposed to other potential technology solutions.

I had one sales opportunity that shows the power of qualifying strongly. On this occasion I was dealing with the New Zealand Customs Service – the equivalent of the US Customs and Border Protection. I had a meeting with a fairly senior decision maker where he seemed very uninterested in using Microsoft technologies and stated this. The reason I met with him is I had heard from another customer that they were looking to go to market through a formal RFP process but hadn't done so yet. I wanted to get the inside running before the "walls" came down in respect to the amount of information I could get due to the strict government procurement process.

Months later the RFI finally came out and I used our USP to position us successfully and we were shortlisted to the RFP stage. To be honest I was quite surprised given the early conversation I had had. So, I decided to contact the main contact on the RFI – a different person to whom I had earlier met – as I was on the fence about responding to the full RFP. It was a huge amount of work which I did not want to do if we had absolutely no chance due to the technology. When I rang her and explained the earlier meeting I had had, and his comments around Microsoft and that I was questioning whether we should respond to the RFP, I could hear the panic in her voice. It was at that moment I realized we must have been at the top of their shortlist and had every chance of winning. She assured me that they were interested in the technology and gave the reason why we were shortlisted which was primarily our USP which was based on our unique approach to developing software, not the technology itself. As it turned out we won the RFP which was a big win for the company I worked for. The information I got over the phone that day was invaluable and shaped how we responded to the RFP and our presentation. It was a great lesson for me in qualifying hard, as there really is nothing to lose and a lot to gain.

Exercise

If you don't already have one, write up a qualification criteria or list of information you need in order to qualify an opportunity. This will be your qualification process and used on every opportunity. As you become proficient this will become second nature but at the start, I highly recommend you have a list to tick off each of the qualification points. This will bring rigor and discipline to the qualification process and eliminate any possibility that you will spend precious time and resources on an unqualified opportunity that never eventuates. It will also help with prioritization and where you should spend the most effort.

Chapter 7

The Sales Process – Presenting

At this stage of the sales process you have progressed your opportunity through the sales funnel and now have a qualified opportunity at the presentation stage. Just like many steps in the sales process it is not really that linear. For example, you might have some amount of "presenting your offering" on your first phone call as well as your first meeting. However for this example we are assuming you have a text book opportunity where you first contacted them, set a meeting where you went through the Discovery process to understand their needs and are now presenting back in a second meeting based on your understanding of their needs and how your solution will best meet these.

Before the meeting you will have done a second wave of research based on the information you gained at the first meeting. This could include any competitors they mentioned so you can understand at a very high level what their key strengths and weaknesses are against your offering. You will now understand their buying process and key decision-makers and influencers and research these people on LinkedIn and any industry specific resources available to you. You will also have a much clearer idea of their needs and the solution that will best help them. The presentation is your opportunity to show that you understand and to pitch not only your solution but your company and your team.

Understanding their drivers

At this stage you will also hopefully understand what the key drivers are for the decision-makers and what's propelling them to make a change. Adapting your pitch to what matters most to them will be more persuasive and also make you come across like you understand them, which is what everyone wants to feel – to be understood. I've seen it many times where the successful company was the one that personalized their pitch to the company or person they were selling to. The degree in which you can do this will vary but try to do it as much as you can. I remember being told a story about an Advertising Agency pitching to a car manufacturer client and the presentation was set up at a destination to showcase their latest model car. On the way the car executives drove past broken down cars of their biggest rival, so their hearts were won by the time they had arrived and before the presentation had even begun.

The Power of a Story

The most effective way to get an idea across to someone is through a story. Humans make decisions on a combination of facts and emotion but what drives us is emotion. If you can combine the two you have a very persuasive tool – the power of a story. Success in story telling is in its simplicity, so that it delivers the message powerfully imbued with emotion. By containing both logic and emotion you are also catering to two different types of people who will lean more to one or the other in their decision-making process, but *both* will be driven by emotion. When I arrived in Hollywood, I was in the epicenter of storytelling but hadn't quite mastered the simplicity I needed for my own pitch. I could feel that how I was delivering the message was too complex and not cutting through.

It wasn't until I got feedback from a customer that had used our technology and they shared with me some of their results. They had literally been able to reduce their shooting schedule for one scene from four days down to one and a half days. Time in the movie industry is money. When I shared this as a simple story, I saw the lights come on in people eyes. What a difference that made.

You may be selling something that is quite complex, and you will need to distill this. Even a technical audience appreciates a story so they can understand how the technology or solution can be applied. All the facts in the world won't tell them that.

Humor

Humor goes a long way to break the ice and make you relatable. People will warm to you much quicker with some humor injected into a meeting. Humor relaxes people and can be quite disarming. For a lot of people when they know they are about to be sold they will put up a defensive barrier to protect themselves from being sold. Bringing humor into the presentation will quickly bring that mental barrier down and make them more open to suggestion. Another positive side effect is it will relax you too! I remember being very nervous at a presentation to a team of top studio executives and while I was waiting for them to arrive, I was talking with the people in the room. One thing led to another and the next moment we were laughing. By the time the execs arrived I had a smile on my face and was feeling very relaxed which carried through to my body language and energy for the meeting, including those in the room that were laughing with me too.

The Power of Conviction

You need to be sold to sell well and people want to see that. As I mentioned in Chapter 3 you have to have a strong belief that you are offering exceptional value. This belief pours out of you, putting people at ease and it's also very persuasive in its own right. Understanding your point of difference in the market will build your conviction. In each sales role I have been in I am completely convinced of the value I can bring to a customer and always shocked if they don't buy from me and very frustrated. This is because I have taken the time to fully understand the USP and convinced that I have the best offering in the market and the customer is making the wrong decision. You can't fake conviction which is why it's so powerful.

Use their name

Someone's name is golden to them so use it as much as possible. When you are presenting look at people directly and use their names. They will love you for it. If you find it difficult to remember names, make sure to repeat their name when they first introduce themselves to you for example "Hi Sarah nice to meet you" and repeat again in your head. Another strategy is name association. For example, if you have a friend called Sarah, thinking of your friend will bring forward her name in your mind. Remembering what you associate with that person's name will help you to recall it. People love to hear their names and it will help you to connect more quickly with people.

Visual presentation

For many presentations there will be a visual element either a PowerPoint or a demo. If using PowerPoint keep slides simple, the less words the better and imagery seems to convey the emotional content of a message more effectively than words. What I find works best is a simple visual slide that is talked to. This also keeps the focus on you. If there are a lot of words on a slide people will instinctively try to read them and at that moment, they are not looking at you or listening to what you are saying. Less is definitely more when it comes to visual presentations.

If you have a demo make sure to tailor it as much as possible before the presentation. If this is not possible tailor the *way* you demo to the client's situation. Personalize as much as possible using language that they understand, not your own, and avoid industry acronyms. If you have research on your customers' customers use their names and include scenarios that are relevant to them. It's amazing how we can all forget what it is like to be in someone else shoes learning about our company, product or offering for the first time. Every time you demo or present imagine yourself in their shoes and talk as if they know nothing – unless of course they do and adjust accordingly! The golden rule is to always personalize your presentation and pitch to your audience.

Body language

As I mentioned in chapter 5 body language communicates much more to someone than words. This extends to how you project your voice. Projecting your voice communicates confidence and if you are presenting to a roomful of people this is important. The only time I would deviate would be if you are presenting one on one where mirroring the person would be more beneficial. For example, if the person you are presenting to is softly spoken lower your own voice to match and vice versa. Mirroring the tone, speed of speech and projection will help build rapport and put someone at ease.

If you are presenting to a roomful of people, make sure you make eye contact with everyone in the room. It's easy to fall into a trap of making eye contact with the most senior or the person we subconsciously relate to the most. Try to be very conscious about it and make eye contact with everyone so they all feel important. You don't know how much influence an individual person may have, even if they are not the final decisionmaker.

As you present looks for signs of engagement. If you see a yawn speed up and move on. If you see people lean forward, linger. Smile, be excited about what you have to say and say it with conviction.

Exercise

Do you have an engaging story? If not, think about the USP you came up with in the earlier exercise in chapter 3. How can you relay that USP in a story? Do you have customer stories or examples you can use? Do you have something that you have experienced personally that you can tell as a story? Finally, once you have a list of stories you can present, try them out either in a sales presentation or as a roleplay. See what reaction you get. Are you pitching it at the right emotional level with the facts? Use this exercise to create stories that deliver your message succinctly and in an engaging way.

Chapter 8

The Sales Process – Proposal

At the end of the presentation the ideal scenario is the customer will ask about costs (a sign they are interested) and ask you to provide them with a proposal. If they don't ask and pricing has been discussed, ask them if they would like a proposal. The purpose of every interaction is to progress to the next step. However, there may be times where it will take longer for you to get to the proposal stage or it happens sooner as their need is urgent. Whatever the case may be, preparing a proposal is an important milestone in the sales process.

As a general rule try to keep language straightforward and easy to understand and avoid acronyms if possible. If it's more practical to use an acronym always write it in full the first time it appears in the body of the proposal. Try to find the balance between persuasiveness in your language tone and sticking to the facts and being concise. A proposal will be read by many different types of people and you are trying to appeal to them all. To that end the proposal should start at a higher level and get more detailed as it progresses. Taking this approach should also help with how you present each part of your proposal.

Finally, and probably most importantly, write the proposal from the customer's perspective. Whenever you are describing a solution write it in terms of how it will work for them based on their needs. Where you have specific knowledge of their needs personalize the description, so it reads like you understand their problem and have designed a specific solution for them. There is nothing worse than reading a proposal where the vendor name is mentioned all over the document and much more so than the client's name. Try and reverse it if you can. You want the customer to be reading their name repeatedly, so they feel a sense of ownership with your proposal.

Whilst the content of proposals will differ slightly depending on the industry, all good proposals have a number of key elements in common:

Executive Summary/introduction

This is where you summarize the key aspects of your proposal and highlight your major point of difference. Any company information or background especially if it feeds into your point of difference should also be here. Personally, I like to keep this to one page if possible two pages at most, even for larger responses to more formal RFP's. If it's well-written and presenting only a summary of the most important parts of your proposal and what really sets you apart, you should really only need two pages.

Solution and/or Approach

This is where you can go into more detail about your proposed solution. Start with the broader concepts before drilling down into the details. Again, always write with the customers' needs and perspective in the forefront. There are of course some pieces of content that are consistent from customer to customer where a copy and paste is OK but try to write original content that targets their needs specifically whenever it makes sense to do so.

Pricing

Some pricing is straightforward and easy to present clearly, whilst some pricing is complex and more difficult to present on a page. If that's the case take the time to think about the best way to present your pricing so that it's simple and easy to understand. If it's too complex it will put off buyers. If it's hard to present or explain your pricing, it might be time for a pricing review.

Another note on pricing. From the many debriefs I have done over the years with formal RFP's the feedback around pricing is that too low can sometimes be just as bad as too high. On some RFP's they have taken out the top and bottom to shortlist, as they didn't believe the bottom was sustainable. Pricing strategy is specific to your industry and the evolution and stage of your business in the market; however, this is a note of caution in attempting to win business on price alone.

Summary & Next Steps

This will be the last thing they read and should leave them with a last positive note and what to expect if they progress with your proposal.

Case studies or customer examples

Case studies or customer examples and references are a great way to build credibility. You can either pepper them throughout the proposal to support the content that it relates to, or you can place them at the end. If you do place them through the body of the proposal you can always end with a logo page highlighting your highest profile customers which will give weight and scale to your proposal and business.

If you have struck the right balance with your proposal you will get feedback similar to "thanks it was easy to read and understand." Whenever I get this feedback, I know I'm onto a winner proposal!

Presenting your proposal

If you can, the ideal situation is to present your proposal in person. Sometimes this is not always possible so an email with a follow-up phone call to talk through is second best. Often, I will email before the meeting, so they have time to review before providing feedback in person which usually makes the meeting more productive and likely to lead to a next step.

Take a copy for each person that you are meeting with and a couple spare just in case people come to the meeting that you are not expecting. Go through the proposal with them, highlighting the key points in each section and make sure you pause for feedback and questions. Be sure to present the proposal in their terms, in other words the value they will get and personalized to their situation. The more you engage and the more they are asking questions and discussing your proposal the better. Try to make it as conversational as possible and as you are talking observe body language and look for signs of engagement. A great way to finish is to ask them a high level question such as "what are your thoughts on what you've seen so far" to get a gauge of their level of interest. This statement will sometimes bring up objections that have been lurking in the back of their mind. This is positive progress and we will cover how to deal with these in the next chapter.

Quality Control

A final note on quality control. With every type of interaction, the customer is evaluating you and deciding whether they can trust you to deliver the solution or service they need. Having a well-written, laid out and professionally presented proposal with no grammatical or spelling errors is important to give the right impression – that you are on top of your game and professional to deal with. At each step of the sales process small errors can add up to a negative perception. In most situations you are competing against other providers and they are evaluating you against them, you don't want to lose points on anything that is easily preventable.

I learnt this lesson the hard way. When I was a Business Development Manager in corporate travel, an insurance company contacted me who I had previously met and developed a relationship with. They had decided to go to market for their travel provider and I met with them and the meeting went extremely well. They asked me to put a proposal together which I did and set up a second meeting to present. This meeting also went well, and I left them with the two copies of the proposal. About an hour after I left, I got a phone call from one of the two people I had met, and she was confused. She had started reading through my proposal and noticed that another company's name was consistently appearing not theirs. I immediately recognized what I had done – I had printed out another company's proposal at the same time and had not double checked when collating and binding that I had the correct version. I had assumed that since the cover was correct so was the body of the proposal. Somehow, I had gotten the two mixed up over the printer. You can imagine how horrified I was and immediately met with her to give her a corrected copy. I knew I was on the backfoot and was furious with myself for letting such a simple error slip by me.

As it turned out we were shortlisted to reference stage so I thought I may have managed to retrieve the opportunity from the brink. I asked the Account Manager who managed the client relationship of the customer reference we were providing for their contact details – and it turned out that she had given me the wrong number so when they went to contact them, they got through to the wrong person. Needless to say, I did not win that business! I was bitterly disappointed as I had worked on that opportunity for a couple of years and we were in a strong position, but two simple mistakes let us down. Check and triple check.

Exercise

Review your current proposal and see where you can simplify it and personalize the content. Specifically look at the pricing and try to put yourself in your customer's shoes with no knowledge of your pricing and product or services, and gauge how easy is it to understand. If you can get feedback from a customer or third party even better, so you can make sure you are giving yourself the best chance of winning with your proposals.

Chapter 9

The Sales Process – Overcoming Objections

Objections are a sign that the customer is engaged and interested but there is a perceived gap between what they need and what you can offer. It's your responsibility to uncover and fully understand their objections to see if it's a stumbling block to a sale. Being an active listener and listening with intention, communicates to the customer that you are wanting to understand their perspective and find a solution to their problem.

Once you have listened and feel you understand the problem, confirm to them your understanding. Doing this can uncover any other objections not yet discussed. The purpose of this process is to get everything out on the table, so you know exactly what you are dealing with and what you need to address in order to get the sale. To do this effectively you need to have empathy, good listening skills, as well as the ability to articulate the problem in a way the customer understands, avoiding industry jargon unless they are using it.

The next step after the objections are fully understood is to offer solutions. This is where having a creative mindset can help. Some of the best performing salespeople also happen to be excellent problem solvers. By taking the problem solving approach you take on the role of helper rather than seller, which puts you in a stronger position to build trust with the customer.

As you go through each objection confirm with them if your solution will address their concern before you move on. If there are any remaining objections that are still not addressed to their satisfaction, find out if this is something of a high enough priority to them that it would prevent the sale progressing. You need to know if this is a showstopper.

Some objections can be dealt with there and then, but some may take time and that's OK. In fact, sometimes it can be useful as you demonstrate what it's like to do business with you. Being consultative and trying to solve their problem is what you want to convey. Iterations of your proposed solution are fine. This gives you more time to build the relationship as you make tweaks to your offering to make sure it delivers all of the value they are looking for.

Every industry will have some specific objections that are unique to the market and the competitive landscape you are in. It pays to understand this as much as you can so that you are armed with the right information to deal with them as best as possible as they arise. There's nothing worse than the feeling of "Oh I should have said that" after the fact. And sometimes you don't get another opportunity with that particular audience to address it. So, build up an inventory of common objections and a response. For example, in the entertainment industry security around creative IP is paramount and this question will come up often. When I first started our software hadn't gone through a comprehensive third party security assessment, so I had to assure them through other means. As our product and the security assessment process developed so did my response.

Early on in my sales career my attitude was to be frustrated with objections and to glaze over them – or probably more accurately bulldoze over them! This didn't leave the customer feeling heard or understood, and I'm sure must have affected my conversion rate.

As I matured as a salesperson, my approach changed to becoming a problem solver and striving to ensure the customer had the best possible experience, with the best way to achieve this being to really understand them. Uncovering and resolving the objections is part of that process. Do this job well and it will make your job of retaining the business once it's won much easier.

I have also noticed a correlation between how easy it is to win the business with how easy it is to lose it. If the customer has taken their time to fully evaluate your offering to make sure it gives them everything they need, and you have responded in kind to make sure that is the case, you are setting yourself up for a long term business relationship. The opposite can also be true. A quick sale without much due diligence by the customer can mean they haven't done their job properly as a buyer. This isn't necessarily a good thing. It can feel great at the time for you the salesperson, but it will backfire down the track when their expectations are not being met. Because you didn't tease this out during the sales process you are running into the transaction blind. Do yourself a favor and make sure you uncover all of their requirements and possible objections to set up the customer and your business for success.

Exercise

Take a moment to think about how you approach objections. What is your mindset when the customer has an objection? Is it to uncover and problem solve or is to deal with it as quickly as possible so you can close the deal? Be honest with yourself. If it's the latter how can you change your attitude knowing that it will result in a better outcome? As with anything sales related, practice and experience hones your craft. Next time you are in a situation with a customer and they have an objection think about your attitude before you respond. If you shift your mindset from a hurdle to discovery, a different response and outcome will follow.

Chapter 10

The Sales Process – Closing & Negotiating

At this point in the sales process you will have a qualified opportunity, you thoroughly understand their requirements and how your offering meets them, you know who the decision-makers are and the approval process, and you have uncovered and addressed any objections. It's now time to close the deal. So how do you get from overcoming their objection to closing a deal? The most seamless way I have found is to use the details of the sale or next steps. This is also referred to as an assumptive close, but I find that description sounds more deceptive than it really is. Let me give you an example. Let's say you are selling photocopy paper. You could ask for the order directly as in "would you like to place an order today?" or you could ask "how may reams of paper do you need?" It's a subtle difference but the latter feels more natural and conversational. It also happens to be an open question that invites a response and not a yes/no answer. If you get a no from the first question it leaves you little room for further conversation.

Let's try another example. This time you are selling professional accounting services to a property developer. You could ask "would you like to go ahead with our services for the 2021 tax year?" or you could say "our top property accounting specialist has availability to start work with you on May 1 if that suits?"

It's like a trial close and if they have not decided yet, this will be uncovered in their response. I find it's a much softer way of closing a sale. It also means you are diving straight into the detail of the sale and driving to fulfillment in a very seamless way.

Another approach is to provide them with options and ask

which they prefer. The options could be price based so they can choose which pricing model suits them best, or it could be solution or delivery based; for example, would you like that color, size or service etc. Again, this is closing using the detail of the sale without asking directly. For example, you have presented a proposal for digital marketing services and given two pricing options; one is a monthly subscription and one is a cost per project. You could ask "which pricing model works best for you?" If they have mentally decided to go with you, they will say which one they want, and the conversation will naturally go down the path of the detail to complete the sale.

If you have a single pricing option but included other solution options, then ask which option they prefer to take you to the same conclusion. It's really that simple. My only caveat would be careful with how many options you provide. Too many and it can become too hard for them to decide. Anything that creates delay can contribute to uncertainty in the buyers' mind and potentially introduce unknown factors that could derail the sale. Time is not your friend when it comes to closing. Try to avoid anything that slows down the decision-making process including difficult to understand options or too many options. Think McDonald's menu.

Part of closing is negotiating and the ideal negotiation is a win/win result with each party very happy with the outcome. For some deals it will be straightforward – the price is the price and the customer accepts it, but for others there will be some "haggling" involved. If you are new to sales and negotiating, this part of the sales process may feel uncomfortable but if you follow a few tips it needn't be.

Have a goal
Before you meet with someone where you know there will be a price discussion or negotiation have a goal of what you would like to get out of the meeting. This will include what you hope

to achieve and what is your bottom line.

Aim high

Whatever your goal is in terms of what you want to achieve, start **above** that. It is very unlikely that you will hit your goal if you start there – the person you are dealing with would have to accept your first offer. So, if you are serious about achieving your goal aim high and start the negotiation at a level that gives you a chance to finish at what you hope to achieve. However, remember that you want to achieve a win/win outcome so keep that in mind. If you aim *too* high you could be perceived negatively by the other party, you want to come across as fair in order to achieve the best outcome for everyone involved. The market talks so you want to avoid being perceived as expensive or difficult to deal with through your negotiations.

Understand the drivers of who you are dealing with

Research the company and the person you are dealing with so that you have a thorough understanding of what their drivers are and what's important to them. You can then apply concessions in the negotiation that are more valuable to them to achieve the desired outcome.

Have a negotiation strategy

This is where your research feeds into your negotiation strategy. Your strategy is another way of saying the stance you will take. For example, if you are dealing with someone who is primarily concerned with reducing risk then your negotiations will focus on how your solution addresses that and a concession might be a value add that reduces risk in the deal or the solution.

Helicopter view

Have a helicopter view of the situation and all of the parties involved. What's going on in all of their situations that could affect their position and how they approach a negotiation? This in turn can affect the approach you take and the negotiation strategy or stance.

She who speaks first loses

Once you make an offer be quiet and wait for a response. Silence can be uncomfortable for some but it's a very useful tool. If you ask the question and don't wait for them to respond you have just let them off the hook and lost precious ground. By staying silent they are compelled to respond and you can understand what their position is. The opposite is true. If you speak first, you will undermine your own position and may reveal information that enhances theirs. And you might just have lost the one opportunity to close the deal.

People need room to think so give them the room they need. Make silence after a question a habit and you'll be amazed at the difference it makes. Silence really is golden.

Be prepared to walk away

You have made your bottom line so be prepared to walk away if the negotiations go below it. It's all in your attitude. If your body language and vocal tone communicate uncertainty or a willingness to drop, the other person will sense this and negotiate accordingly. If there is a deal to be done it will happen and if it's not, then you have avoided a win/lose negotiation. I remember learning this lesson in my early 20's on a shopping trip. I walked into a shop and was very undecided about a jacket which for me at the time was an expensive purchase. I ummed and aahed and was about to leave the shop when the business owner started dropping the price. I was still uncertain, and she dropped the price further. It got to a point where it was so low that I accepted and purchased the jacket. It was a learning experience for me in human behavior and to not be too emotionally invested in an outcome. Essentially be prepared to walk away.

Once you have agreement stop selling

This is much like the "she who speak first loses" principle but for a different reason. Sometimes you can unravel all of your good work after the fact. Once you have agreed and closed the deal go through the sale details but do not keep selling. This can make people feel uneasy and question their decision. Psychologically speaking why would you be selling if it's already been sold? To avoid any doubt in the buyer's mind do not make any comments about how good the product is or how pleased they will be with their purchase, just complete the sale process and leave it at that.

A note on discounting

It's always best to sell on value wherever possible and to avoid discounting. I understand this is not always possible and different industries have different expectations around this. My first business to business sales role was with the Yellow Pages in Australia where there was no discounting allowed. I was unable to discount period. That set me up well to sell on value and not to default to discounting to get the sale. Over time if overused discounting can become a default habit and rob you off significant margin needlessly. If you take the above negotiation steps and apply them, you will hopefully avoid this pitfall.

Exercise

Take a current opportunity or if you prefer a past negotiation and apply the principles above. Write down your goal for the negotiation and your bottom line. Then research the company and person you will be dealing with so that you understand their drivers and write these down. Next apply a strategy or stance that you will take in the negotiation that is based on your understanding of their drivers.

If you can roleplay the negotiation with someone who can represent the buyer and share with them your knowledge of their drivers, but do not divulge your goal or bottom line. You are trying to replicate a negotiation that is as close to reality as possible. Apply the key principles from above from closing using the "assumptive close" approach through to negotiation and using all of the tips especially the golden silence. Get feedback from the other person and keep practicing. The more you practice the more natural and habitual it will become.

Chapter 11

The Sales Process – Follow-up & Building Relationships

Now that you have completed the sale you will want to develop the customer into a long term business relationship with ongoing sales. The very first step to achieving this is excellent follow-up. Follow-up is the key to long term sales success and is required at every milestone. The first milestone after the sale is delivery. Once that is complete you will want to follow-up after a certain period to ensure that the solution or service meets all of their expectations. Getting feedback is important for multiple reasons. It gives you an opportunity to interact with the client and every interaction builds the relationship. You will also get invaluable feedback that you can use to improve your product or service not just for this client but for other clients and help with building further opportunities through an improved offering. Feedback can also include competitor information that can be invaluable in understanding the competitive landscape. Finally, you will get information from the client that could lead to another sale. The sales cycle is in essence a continuous loop.

A marriage

Sometimes the feedback is not what you were hoping to hear. The customer's expectations may not have been met and you are responsible for fixing that. On the surface this can be seen as a negative but on the occasions I have been through this, it almost always results in a stronger relationship – much like a marriage that has come through a rocky patch and come out the other end stronger for it.

If you take the attitude that the customer is always right

when it comes to *perception*, then it will be a much smoother process to resolution. Even if you have a solid, logical reason why their expectations weren't met, customer perception is what matters most. For example, let's say they were not using a product correctly, until you have changed their perception, your offering does not meet their needs. As a result, they are unlikely to recommend you to others and more likely to tell other people of their negative experience. This is why follow-up is so vital. You need to both capitalize on the good experience and mitigate the bad.

The effort you go to in rectifying the situation with the client will directly affect the state of the relationship after the negative experience. It's quite possible with concerted effort to fix the issue that the client will become a loyal customer as a result and become a strong advocate. They also make the perfect referee as this is a common question in reference checking, "how does the company respond when things don't go as planned." Having a customer that can answer that question with a specific example and show how you made a wrong right is priceless.

On the other hand, you also want to know when you have done a great job! And like I mentioned earlier you really want to capitalize on that. This comes in a number of ways – through becoming a referrer to other businesses and generally being your advocate in the market, being a reference customer if this is required, or being part of a marketing campaign or case study/customer story. All of these will build your business and profile in the market. And most importantly with good follow-up and a positive experience you might get another opportunity with the same client. The cost of sale is much lower with repeat business than developing a new customer and usually the time to close the deal much less.

Advocates

When building relationships either inside existing accounts or even in business development within a new account, you will sometimes find an "advocate." This is the person who really understands the value you bring and wants to promote you internally within the company. When this happens, you want to arm them with everything they need to sell your company and to respond to their requests quickly and efficiently so that you make their job of selling you easy.

The traditional thinking of growing an account is to "go high and wide." What this means is that you go as high as you can in the hierarchy of the company and across all of the business units to make sure you understand the potential opportunity for sales overall and ensure you have included all decision-makers and influencers across the company structure. However, there is a different approach that can sometime work extremely well. This is when you have an advocate that yields considerable influence and has the knowledge and savvy to navigate the company's internal decision-making process on your behalf. In this situation if you have a competent and influential person on the client side, you can literally "ride their coat tails" to sales success. The one caveat with this approach is that you have to be confident that the person is both capable AND influential inside the organization. It's a high risk approach in that you are putting all your eggs in one basket so to speak, instead of going high and wide. But if you are confident that this person displays both the smarts and influence then it can be a very successful sales strategy.

When I was working for the software development company in New Zealand, I took this approach on two occasions that resulted in two significant wins. The first was a major bank that used our company on an adhoc basis for small web projects, when they didn't have the capacity in-house. When I was meeting with our main contact for this account, he mentioned casually in passing about an "online store." My ears pricked up as I realized this must be a potential new project and asked who was driving this internally and he gave me a name. I picked up the phone that day and set up a time to meet with the contact. After meeting him for an initial chat he was interested to see how we could help. This was a new innovation and first for the banking sector, until that point e-commerce was associated with traditional retail and if successful would be a high profile project for this person. Because of our agility we could ramp up quickly and get an MVP (Minimum Viable Product) live, well before their own internal team could. I could see that my client contact was very quick and responsive and was driving the internal decision-making process at a senior level. I decided to "ride his coat tails" as I could see he was quite capable of driving the sale process internally. We won the deal to build the first iteration of the "Online Store" as it was called and this account subsequently grew into our largest client at that time, billing six figures every month over multiple years. All from that one phone call.

The other time was for the New Zealand Defence Force who were looking to move from an in-house model with vendor supplied contractors to supplement their software development team, to a full outsourcing model where the vendor owned the outcome. It just so happened that a contact from an existing customer had become a consultant driving the project and had the ears of the most senior people in the decision-making process. Given it was a highly secure environment with a large bureaucracy I again opted to go with the "ride the coat tails" strategy. I did all that I could to make his job easy to sell us internally and as a previous customer he knew our strengths and was able to articulate these. As it was a government account, we went through a formal procurement process or Request for Proposal (RFP) that required a written response and presentation. Throughout the process I was largely led by the client on our approach, due to his knowledge and understanding of the account and decision-making process. He wanted us to win as much as we did and we ultimately won what was a very large account. It became our largest account at that point – bigger than the bank.

These are just two examples among many more traditional sales approaches and it certainly is the exception rather than the rule. However, if you do find yourself working with the type of individual where you feel this approach could be successful, from my own experience it's most definitely worthwhile.

Lead with innovation

After the first follow-up after a sale you will want to nurture the relationship and grow the opportunities with the customer. If you have sold something that has ongoing revenue this is more straightforward. There is generally an expectation that they will have an Account Manager or some sort of visit and representation from your company to ensure that they continue to get value and their expectations are being met. However, if you have sold something that is considered a "one-off" or project related where the need is for a fixed period, it can sometimes be difficult to reengage and keep the relationship going so that you are top of mind for future opportunities.

What I have found for both these scenarios – Business Development and ongoing Relationship/Account Management – is that leading with innovation is the most effective way to reengage and recapture a customer's attention.

With a rapidly evolving marketplace it's important to remain relevant and the only way to do that is innovate. Innovation helps to establish an even stronger USP and drive sales. If you are a business owner, you are in the ideal position to make this happen and drive the innovation platform for your sales expansion. If you are a salesperson you too can lead with innovation to drive sales. It's just a matter of engaging your best and brightest minds in your company to help create the solution or service that will lead the market. As a salesperson you have market insights that only a salesperson can gain from so many customer conversations and you need to take this back to your team to feed into product strategy. This strategy is focused on delivering innovation to drive sales. Innovation is a gift to salespeople and puts you in an advantageous position. Wherever you can, use it to lead conversations back into old or existing customers to reengage. It's also the best way to keep developing new business.

Innovation can be in one particular area, it doesn't need to be a whole product or service. As long as that aspect gives you an edge over your competition and is an exciting talking point that's all you need. I have had many times where I have got a meeting through leading with innovation and it has opened doors to more traditional business. It's what gets people excited and starting the conversation that counts.

Lastly, like attracts like and what you'll find is that by leading with innovation you will attract the type of customer you enjoy working with. Just as you want to innovate, they want to work with innovative businesses and are more likely to be early adopters. This feeds into your marketing and sales drive as you will have case studies or customer stories early in the innovation cycle.

And while we are discussing case studies and referrals. It pays to set this up early so that you don't have any obstacles later. Plant the seed early on in the sales cycle so that the customer is prepared for what will come later. Even better it can be part of your negotiations to include a published case study. Also, with referrals never be afraid to ask. Obviously, the best ones are ones that come to you without asking directly, but if you know you have done an excellent job the customer is usually only too happy to introduce you to someone else. I sometimes have a particular company or person in mind and ask them if they don't mind introducing me. I will soften it with "or if you like I can contact them and mention your name?" they will either say yes or do the introduction themselves – typically over email.

Striking the balance

I am always conscious of making sure that any follow-up is perceived positively by the client and not seen as annoying. How do you know if you are striking the right balance? The first strategy is to always agree the next step with the client. This could be on a phone call or in a meeting, but every interaction needs to have an agreed next step. What that means is you are keeping your promise by following up and the customer will be expecting your call or email, and will appreciate it. In fact, it will be seen as very proactive and puts you in a positive mindset with the client.

Sometimes it can be difficult to have an agreed next step, for example it's a client who you have called or met but they are not yet actively in the market or ready to make a purchasing decision. However, you want to build the relationship and maintain visibility with them so that when they are ready you will come to mind. To strike the right balance here, you need to be seen to add value with each interaction or follow-up. What I tend to do is to "check-in" but have something to offer that I think will be of interest to the customer at the same time. This could be a new development, innovation or product in your business. I will title an email with an interesting title that highlights the new development and provide further information or a next step in the email if they are interested. I will write it so that a response is not necessarily expected but if there is interest, I will have a suggested next step. In this way you are being proactive, offering value and staying connected without being annoying.

Although follow-up is placed at the end of the sales process it's really not that linear. Follow-up is at the heart of sales – follow-up and next steps. If there is only one thing you take from this book and that is to commit to continued follow-up and agreeing next steps, you would have implemented what I think is the most important aspect of effective selling.

I have had situations where a potential client will tell me that they will be buying in a year and I will take notes and contact them a year later to progress the opportunity. I can hear the surprise in their voice when I contact them and reiterate our conversation. It's pretty simple really but makes such a big impact on how well you will sell. Follow-up.

Exercise

Think about how you can lead with innovation. Do you have something currently that is innovative and market leading even if it's just one aspect of your offering? If you do, look at how you can generate interest. This could be a larger marketing campaign or direct emails to specific customers you believe would benefit or at least be very interested in learning about this innovation. Or you could set up an event that is centered on this innovation and generate leads and interest from the event. Use this exercise to brainstorm ideas and approaches to see where you can lead with innovation and use this as your sales tool.

Chapter 12

Sales Debriefs – how to get information & feedback

Now that we have gone through the sales process, we will look at some specific areas that will support your sales efforts. An area that supports the sales approach to a great degree, is how effective you are in getting information and feedback. This can be in a general sense, or in a more formal situation such as a sales debrief following a formal sales evaluation for an RFP or similar.

In order to get information from someone, a lot of the core principles of being influential apply. That is, you need to be likeable, have empathy and social intelligence and watch for cues in body language. The most important thing in relation to getting information is they need to trust you. To do this you need to "disarm with your charm." Everyone has a natural barrier for protection and probably even more so in business situations where people will put on their business persona. You want to appear relaxed, open and warm. On the inside you will be quite different – you will be focused, directed and observing. You need to be this way in order to get them to open up and for you to drive and steer the conversation. It's really no different from a selling situation except now we are 100% focused on getting information. Why is this so important that it deserves its own chapter? Because information is the lifeblood of sales and without it you're driving blind.

As with the discovery stage of the sales process, when you are seeking information or feedback it is best to start at a high level first. This will open up the conversation and also make it appear more conversational and less like an interrogation. Throughout this process you are building trust so that they will share more with you, so employ the reassurances that will enable this such as nodding, smiling and listening with direct eye contact. As you see them feeling more comfortable narrow your questions down into more detail and confirm your understanding after they have finished. What you will find is as they drop their guard with you, they will reveal more, as long as you have established rapport and trust. This approach is best done in person, but you can apply the same principles over the phone if that is your only option.

Formal Debrief

At the end of a formal procurement process there is often an opportunity to do debrief. If one is not offered always ask if you can do this as it is a really valuable exercise. You will get information that you wouldn't otherwise get that you can use to continue to improve. This can feed into the sales process so you can improve how you prepare your proposals, presentations and understand your strengths and weaknesses against your competitors and position accordingly.

Before you meet the person for the debrief write a list of questions you would like to cover off. In general, debriefs are driven by the vendor, as the sole purpose is to give you feedback so it's best that you are prepared. Following the same approach as above, start with the easiest most general questions first before you drill down. You won't be able to prepare all questions as some information that is shared will lead you to ask additional questions and you will get better at this the more debriefs you do. Some questions will be solution/industry specific, but these are a few that you should include:

- How many companies were invited to participate in the RFP?
- How many responded?
- How many were shortlisted?

- What was the main criteria for the shortlist?
- Who was on the shortlist? (they may not give you this information but always ask)
- Where did we rank overall?
- Where were we ranked in pricing?
- What were our strengths?
- What were our weaknesses?
- Were any of our weaknesses a showstopper?
- If there was a showstopper - for the purposes of the debrief if we put that to one side e.g. price was too high, could we have won? (this question will bring out anything else that hasn't yet been uncovered)

What you will find is that the strengths and weaknesses questions will lead to further questions in order to understand these more. But if you ask these at a minimum you will get a wealth of information. Just remember to be very friendly, relaxed and warm whilst directing the conversation. If they have to answer no to a question because they are unable to give you the information, be very supportive of the person. Remember this can be very difficult for them, giving a debrief to someone who has not won at RFP and you want to make them feel comfortable. Even if they can't answer the question you want them to feel like they really want to help you and answer the next.

I've had two memorable debriefs. One was with a woman who could only give me 30 minutes of her time and it was the very first debrief in a new company I worked for in software development. As a result, I was determined to do a good job and came prepared with my list of questions. We were in a busy and loud café so I was super focused to make sure I didn't miss a thing. I went through the questions above but the direction changed as she explained how we were on the shortlist but their requirements changed but our response didn't adapt. I drilled down further to reveal information that we weren't aware of and it was a good learning. After 30 minutes I had got everything I needed and she was off. My CEO commented on the level of detail and learnings captured – not knowing it was all done in 30 minutes!

The other time was when I met with a man who was running a government RFP debrief and as I took the same approach – broader questions and then drill down – he started to add more detail pre-faced with "I would normally never say this but..." the amount of information I got was phenomenal and a direct result of "disarm with charm."

Exercise

Write a list of questions that you can use as a template for debriefs. Include what I have listed but also think about any areas of your offering or industry that you would like to know more about from the customer's perspective and the competitive landscape. Include these specific areas in your questions.

Chapter 13

Selling over the Phone

My very first business to business sales role was telephone sales for the Yellow Pages. I started out with six weeks training and then it was full-time on the phones. I was given an account list of existing advertisers and non-advertisers (they had a "free trade entry") and it was my responsibility to reach a daily margin target in order to increase our revenue for each directory and over the year by a certain percentage. I had to minimize reductions in advertising spend as well as cancellations, increase advertising spend wherever possible and a percentage increase was built into renewals. However renewing only would not reach the target we had to achieve. It was a great experience that was to hold me in good stead for the rest of my sales career. For example, when I was in radio sales we would hold "phone selling days" as a way to hit our end of month target. The radio station sales manager would create a promotion that would entice advertisers and the entire sales team would get on the phone and sell the promotion to existing or new advertisers. I noticed that in most months I would bring in the most revenue over the phone. It was due to the two years at Yellow Pages where I developed solid phone skills. To this day there are still roles that are 100% phone based and even if you're not in a phone sales role, having good sales skills over the phone is a big advantage for any salesperson.

Sales process in a phone call

Selling over the phone might mean you are compressing the sales process into a single phone call. Sometimes the follow-up might take a few phone calls but often I would go through all of the steps from preparing for the phone call, making the call, discovery, presenting, overcoming objections and negotiating and closing all in one phone call. The sales process really does apply to all sales situations, including over the phone. This makes your phone presence vital to how natural this will feel to the customer. Following are some tips that will help.

Be prepared

You need to treat the phone call exactly the same as if you are going to a physical meeting. Do your research before the call and make sure you have everything you may need on the call. Remember, you could be discussing pricing and contract details on this call so have all of that on hand and within easy reach.

Be comfortable

Set yourself up physically that you are comfortable selling over the phone. This may mean you will want a headset so that your hands are free to type or write notes. Just a note here on typing – the person at the other end will hear you tapping on the keyboard and this can be taken as not listening. If you can, write notes and type them up later so there is no misperception on the custome'rs part or any distraction from the conversation.

You also might want to think about whether you want to sit or stand. Some people find standing desks more comfortable and it can also affect your energy and projection. Everyone is different so it's worth noting how you feel standing to sitting when you are on the phone and adjust.

Find a quiet place

With selling over the phone you will need to make sure there is no background noise that can both make it difficult for you to hear and be a distraction to the customer. It just doesn't give a professional impression if there is significant background noise.

Smile

When you smile the tone of your voice changes and that comes through the phone. A tip I got when I first started out in Yellow Pages was to have a mirror on the desk as a reminder to smile. This might be too much for some, but even if you pause for a moment before you pick up the phone to remind yourself to smile. Once you are talking try and lift your voice and vocal tone above what you normally would – the phone will over emphasize any flat or dull tones.

Slow down

As a New Zealander I naturally talk at a faster speed than most! I have had to learn to slow down especially over the phone as there is no body language or lip reading to help people understand what's being said. Also, you will be explaining sometimes fairly complex ideas so you will need to slow down so that people have the time to comprehend. Your communication skills will be extremely important when selling over the phone.

Watch for vocal habits

When I was at Yellow Pages I had a Sales Manager who was able to listen to my calls at any time. This was for sales training and to give advice and guidance. It was quite nerve-wracking knowing he could be listening at any moment, but it was a great learning experience and really helped me improve my phone selling skills. I remember one time after I finished a call, he came up to me and said that it was a great call however I said "right" a lot after I ended sentences and it came across harshly. I hadn't even realized I did this! There may be habitual things you do vocally that in a physical meeting due to body language and having that in-person connection doesn't have any negative impact. But as soon as you have only your voice to connect and build rapport, those small habits can start to detract.

Ask lots of questions

Because there are no visual cues you will need to have many more pauses and opportunities for the other person to speak than you would normally do in person. In fact, this is a great habit for any salesperson whether it's over the phone or in person! If you don't do this, you will be talking with silence at the other end of the phone with no feedback or cues to see if you are on track and engaging them. If you pause frequently you will give them an opportunity to speak which will give you information to keep driving the conversation in the right direction. It also makes it more conversational and natural. As with any sales interaction you never want to find yourself doing most of the talking. To change tack, ask a question, pause and listen.

Repetition

As with anything sales related repetition helps with building skills. The more you engage over the phone and make calls the more comfortable and confident over the phone you will become. If you have a choice to send an email or make a phone call and you don't think the different approach will matter, choose the phone call. Any practice you can get, take it.

When I started working for a graphic design and web development company, I was working in a small rented office with the owners within ear shot. I had to make cold calls with them in the room and although it was quite uncomfortable at the start, I became proficient at making cold calls and setting meetings on the phone in their presence. As the owners I knew they were listening but I learnt to mentally block them out. I became a cold calling machine!

Exercise

If you can, roleplay over the phone with someone and record the conversation. Get the person to take on the persona of a customer that you are selling to and make it as realistic as possible. Practice going through the entire sales process from discovery through to closing and get the person to write down some realistic objections that you will have to respond to. When you are finished get any feedback from the person and also listen back to the call taking note of any areas you feel you didn't come across well. Do this as many times as you feel you need to improve and become more confident on the phone.

Chapter 14

Overcoming Rejection

Sales is the type of role where you will encounter rejection almost daily. The more successful you are the more rejection you will face. The most successful salespeople are a result of high activity + high skill and results come from adding these two ingredients together. But to get to success you will with 100% certainty encounter many situations where your offering/ solution/company will be rejected. As I said earlier this is part of becoming comfortable with being uncomfortable, as most people will never fully be comfortable with rejection. The most important thing is to not let the fear of rejection become a barrier to high activity.

Change your perspective

What I have found most helpful is to have a different view of rejection. Instead of feeling rejected, feel frustrated. Frustrated that you weren't able to convince the customer that you have the best offering and frustrated that they are making a poor decision. This all ties in with being completely sold yourself on your solution – the power of conviction I refer to in chapter 7. As soon as you change to this perspective you become more determined and less affected by a rejection. I have on countless occasions when a customer has chosen a competitor's product or service been **so** frustrated that they cannot see what I see – and I haven't convinced them. I honestly believe they are making the wrong decision. My focus is so much on this, that there is no room for thought of rejection. The benefit that this change of perspective brings is that you are not in the negative emotional state that rejection brings, but on how you can resurrect or save the opportunity. At worst case if the decision is final you will be thinking *next*. Which is exactly where you want to be.

You learn more from No's than Yes's

If there is one silver lining to rejection it's this; isn't it interesting that in my previous chapter on debriefs it was all about learnings from someone saying No not Yes. On the odd occasion when I have won and have asked why, it's usually a one sentence answer from the client with little depth. And that's on the occasion I ask. Mostly I'm too busy congratulating myself and the team, to give serious thought to why we won.

If you get a No, pause to think why and how you can improve next time. This can be to the extent of a full debrief after a formal procurement process or taking the time to think about how you managed a phone call where a client would not make time to meet with you. In that moment go to self-improvement first, there will be no mental space to dwell on rejection.

It's *usually* not personal

In most situations when you get a rejection there will be a reason which could be anything from the solution does not meet their needs to timing. It could even be as trivial as you phoned someone on a bad day so didn't get the meeting! So, it's important to take everything into account and remind yourself it's not personal. As long as you are focusing on continual improvement through self-evaluation, each time you get a no you are one step closer to a yes. However, sometimes it is more personal – you may have said something that steered you off course and made it hard to recover. In that case it's a matter of picking yourself up again, acknowledging what went wrong and think about how to do it better next time. Then make another call.

I remember in my mid 20's when I was selling magazine advertising in Melbourne, Australia I was talking to a jeweler about advertising. As part of the conversation and to build rapport and connect with him, I mentioned the "Diamond

Exchange" in New York and how I would be interested in going there one day. I didn't observe anything negative in his body language at the time, so when I called a few weeks later to follow-up I was surprised when he asked if I was the salesperson that talked about going to the Diamond Exchange. When I said yes he said he would never deal with me after that conversation and hung up. There was no denying this was personal. However, it was a real learning curve for me to be very sensitive to everyone's situation. I realized I had spoken about and showed interest in purchasing from a competitor – an unlikely one in that it was in another country but one nonetheless. If I think about how I would talk to a potential customer now, I am very sensitive to how what I say is perceived and proceed with caution. I also center the conversation around their business and try to put myself in their shoes. That phone call, although very uncomfortable at the time and quite embarrassing was a valuable lesson.

Mental discipline

Changing your perspective and having mental discipline will help prevent the fear of rejection becoming your Achilles heel. When you become down it's a double edged sword. Not only do you not feel motivated and are fearful, but even if you do pull yourself together enough to reach out again, you won't be in the proper mental space to be effective. You need to build mental toughness and resilience. This doesn't happen overnight but with committed effort and disciplining your thoughts you will master them over time. Remember you are not your thoughts. You are the master of your thoughts. Who is observing your thoughts when you are thinking? You. So change your thoughts and perspective and you will find action will follow. Sometimes you just have to have the mental toughness to pick yourself up again and take another step towards your goal.

See the bigger picture

Seeing the bigger picture is also about changing your perspective. If you have just missed out on a big deal look at the bigger picture. Where are you headed and how does this one deal effect that? Although it feels significant right now, if you continue to develop your sales skills and have high activity this will become one loss amongst many wins. Ask yourself; how important will this be in five years' time? It's likely that it won't be as important as it is now. However, the next phone call you make could be the next significant deal that does shape you and your company's future. Not making that phone call could change the outcome. Remember the big picture.

Exercise

Next time you feel yourself being overcome with rejection shift your viewpoint. Allow yourself to feel frustrated with the decision and think if there is any way of changing the outcome. If the decision is final think about what you could have done differently. Do this self-analysis with the view to learning and improving. Being self-aware is an important aspect to performance improvement – be gentle with yourself but honest. Write down your learnings and apply them.

Chapter 15

Staying Motivated

Motivation is a big part of sales as it's largely a self-driven activity. Your level of motivation directly influences your effectiveness, so it pays to monitor your motivation and find ways to keep levels high. For some people myself included, the sense of self-management and freedom that comes with a sales role is part of the attraction. What I have discovered from my experience is that discipline = freedom. Through discipline we achieve the freedom we desire. In my early days I was driven by the need for freedom and didn't like structure all that much and lacked self-discipline. Over the years I worked out that by applying myself consistently, I achieved results that in turn gave me more freedom.

Before motivation you have inspiration. In my 30's I sang Jazz and took piano lessons from an accomplished Jazz pianist who also taught me songwriting. At the time I lived in Wellington, New Zealand in a cottage on the waterfront and she suggested before I sit down to write songs that I go for a walk along the coastline. She knew that I needed to be inspired to be creative. It's the same for selling. You need to be inspired to be motivated. What inspires you? What is your life's dream? These are big questions, but just as some of the most successful companies have a written vision, so we all need our own life vision. This becomes our compass from which we can set goals and keep our motivation high.

I currently have a written vision for how I want my life to look and goals that feed into that vision. This gives me the motivation to get up each morning and do the activity I need to do to reach my goals and ultimately live my vision. It also helps to break the goals down into smaller goals so that they are achievable, and you can experience success early on which again feeds your motivation.

Persistence

Sometimes you just need to persevere to get where you want to be. The bigger your vision and goals, the more persistent you will need to be. I have had "cry in my hands" moments especially soon after I arrived in the US and had many obstacles. What kept me going is probably two things. First is I knew that what I was trying to achieve was difficult – and if it wasn't then everyone would be doing it. Second is I knew that if anyone could do it I could. Knowing those two things was enough sustenance to get me through. I would apply myself daily and never give up. I knew in my heart of hearts that activity + skill = success and I had both. I also knew that the technology I was selling was unique and at the forefront of innovation, so it was just a matter of time – this gave me the determination to persist despite the obstacles.

Overcoming obstacles

Sometimes despite your best efforts you will have obstacles that at the time seem unsurmountable. But I can say from personal experience that if you keep applying yourself with a level of self-awareness so you continue to learn and improve and apply all of the sales principles I have given you – you will succeed. Sometimes sheer determination will get you over the line – as long as you continue to do the activity *and* skillfully.

The biggest obstacle I have faced in my sales career was breaking into Hollywood. I was selling a niche production technology that had very entrenched incumbents and studios and creatives that were risk averse and wary of change. To make it even more difficult there were a lot of influencers and not an identifiable single decision maker. The first part of the sales process was to remove the potential barriers – the influencers who could say no and stop the sale from progressing any further. These people were numerous and getting their support although imperative did not guarantee a sale, only remove the barrier. As you can imagine this was a painstakingly slow process and it took me five months to get my first small sale on a low budget production.

In the first year I could count my sales on one hand. I kept going and kept making the calls and doing the demo's as I knew the technology we had was world class and truly innovative. Over time we stopped being the industry newcomer from the other side of the world, we were on their radar and being talked about. It took two years to get to the point where we were getting month on month sales revenue increase. This was by far the most challenging experience and the slowest. Up until then the longest sales cycle I had experienced was two years for a large multi-million dollar deal with the New Zealand government. That sale in comparison now seemed quite straight forward.

Some days of course I would not feel like doing what I needed to do. But I did it anyway. I knew that once I started I was away, pursuing new sales opportunities and progressing what was already in the pipeline to make sure I gave myself the best possible chance of success. I would wake up each morning and have my vision and inspiration in my mind and knew what I was here to do and why, which gave me the drive to do it.

Creating habits

We have talked about inspiration and motivation – the action derived from inspiration. Part of maintaining motivation is developing productive habits. Habits form a disciplined structure to your day to keep you moving in the direction of your goals. Good habits then become your default behavior so that even when you have headwinds such as a bad night of sleep, additional personal or work stress or frustrating delays, your default habits will keep you in forward motion. Day after day.

And just like an interest bearing bank account that starts with a small balance and over time grows to a significant amount, so good habits create the same effect over time. One of my favorite habits that I learnt early on from another senior salesperson giving me advice as a young 20 year old, was when I thought I was finished for the day just make one more call. I love this habit. Try it next time and see how you feel. Many times, that last call will be a very productive one. If you add up that one extra call a day over time it amounts to a significant accrual of productivity that will have an impact. It might not be a call, it could be an email or whatever activity you are doing, but when you feel like you are done for the day, do one more thing – and watch your productivity and results grow.

Prioritization

It might seem odd to be talking about prioritizing as part of staying motivated, but I've found it a useful tool. Do you remember the last time you looked at a list of things to do and how some things on the list inspired you less than others? Take another look at that list and look at the items that are the most likely to bring you closer to your goals and living your vision. Do you feel more motivated to complete these tasks on your list? My guess is yes. And that's how effective prioritization can keep you motivated on a daily basis.

Start prioritizing your "to do" list daily, ideally it's the first thing you do before you start your day. Bring to the top those tasks that are most likely to progress towards a sale or your goals. And if there is anything on the list that does not contribute to your goals and vision ask yourself why is it there. Prioritizing daily will make you more effective and get results faster through completion of the most important tasks. It's a continuous positive cycle that supports productive daily habits and keeps motivation high.

Exercise

Write a vision for your life in the present tense. It should cover the key areas of your life that are important to you and be no longer than a few sentences. It should make you feel excited and energized when you read it and something that you can believe in. Read this every day.

Chapter 16

Managing your Energy

Sales can be demanding both mentally and physically and we need adequate levels of energy to stay in peak performance. Energy is not infinite and has to be managed so it's not depleted below what you need to be vital. Much like a bank account you have an energy "account." This energy account needs to be replenished to keep reserves high enough for you to lead a full and productive life.

I've learnt this the hard way and have experienced "burn out" in my working life. The cause of this primarily is not listening to my body and continuing to push myself without putting anything back in the tank. The first time I experienced this I was in my mid 30's a single mum, working as Business Development Manager for a corporate travel company and singing and managing a jazz band in the evenings and weekends. My life was full, but I was not listening to my body and pushing myself too hard. It got to the point where I would wake up in the morning with my head feeling like it was a heavy brick and I could barely get it off the pillow. It was sheer will-power that got me out of bed every day. Eventually what saved me was a year and a half of working 20 hours a week and spending two days a week writing music. This was a restorative time of my life where I felt inspired and often lost in my music and in "The Zone." I recall being told by a client that I was the most chilled out Account Manager they had ever encountered. I remember being worried at the time that I was not coming across professional enough but looking back I realize I was just very relaxed yet engaged. This was from balancing my time between working and doing something I loved. Just like the bank account I was putting in as much and probably more than I was taking out. During this time, I created a lot of habits that I have kept to this day that have helped me keep my energy and prevent burn-out.

Managing your schedule

You need to be the owner of your schedule and make sure you schedule time for yourself. This may mean you need to block out time so that it is not scheduled by other people in order to make time for yourself. Creating work/life balance is a conscious effort and it won't happen by accident. If you don't make yourself a priority no-one else will.

How you start your day can make a big difference. For many people, the first thing they will do when they open their eyes is to reach out and grab their phone and check emails, news sites and social media. This is a digital onslaught before you have even got out of bed! Not to mention setting you up on high alert depleting your mental energy.

During the time I mentioned in my mid 30's I started meditating on a daily basis in the morning. I found it made me relaxed, happy and with a spring in my step to start the day. I also walked daily for exercise along the waterfront and over the Wellington hills. This physical activity was energizing and being out in nature was uplifting and inspiring. These three things alone were putting many deposits into by energy account! Schedule these into your day. You don't have to be working only 20 hours a week to make this achievable. Wake up 30 minutes earlier, meditate for 10 minutes and exercise for 20. That's achievable on a daily basis.

Mindfulness

Have you ever travelled to a new city or country and been completely enthralled? You know that feeling of taking in everything that is new, the sights, sounds and energy of a new place. The reason it's so captivating and feels so good is that you are fully present in the moment. The sensory overload is such that you are forced to take it all in and be fully present. This is mindfulness and it's quite energizing whilst relaxing to the nervous system.

Mindfulness or meditation is deeply restorative and can help maintain energy levels. There are many resources that you can find through books, courses and even Apps that can help to teach you various techniques for mindfulness and meditation. I would highly recommend researching these and developing a daily habit even if it's just for five minutes a day. Even individual moments in a day where you turn your attention to the present can be very effective in calming and relaxing the mind, which helps with energy levels and productivity.

Microbreaks

In the past in my working career I've sometimes got so busy and felt that I cannot stop to have a break. This then becomes a never-ending cycle of working without a physical and mental break and overtime I became less effective. I would know this as eventually I would have a holiday and when I came back, I realized I was getting through so much more work much more effortlessly. That told me that the concept of working without breaks was actually counterproductive.

The next time you find yourself falling into this pattern take what I call a microbreak. Try not to go more than two hours without some sort of break and a microbreak of five minutes at a minimum. With the microbreak be sure to make the break both physical and mental. For example, take a walk outside to get some fresh air so that you are moving your body and you are removing yourself from your work environment. This is also an opportunity to be more mindful and really relax your brain. Look at the trees outside and notice how the branches and leaves move in the wind. What sounds can you hear? Can you hear the wind, birds or the sounds of traffic and pedestrians? If this is a coffee break, drink the coffee slowly and really taste it and feel the sensations of the hot drink in your hands and drinking it. Be present in whatever you are doing in your microbreak to maximize the benefit to your mind and nervous system. Give yourself the gift of the present.

Do something you love, some of the time

If you are one of the fortunate ones this won't be difficult as your chosen profession is something you love. But for a lot of people this is not the case. There will be elements of your job that are enjoyable, but it wouldn't be described as something you love. If this is you, it's important to inject your life with something you love doing to bring balance and vitality to your life. Without this your energy account will be depleted over time.

I loved music and singing which was my outlet, but it could be anything from volunteering for your favorite charity to reading a good book. Whatever brings you energy when you do it make sure you do it at least weekly. It's important to strive towards goals and have persistence and work ethic but if that's all you have your life won't be as full as it could be. Often, it's the simple things in life that bring us great joy that ironically are often the first things to go when we are hyper-focused on our goals. Don't let that happen to you, ultimately the journey takes up more time than reaching the destination so you might as well make the ride as enjoyable as possible!

Listen

As the owner of your mind, spirit and body you are best placed more than anyone to know what you need to maintain your energy and vitality. As much as I can write suggestions here, they are just that, suggestions and you have the inner resource to know what's best for you. Being observant of your own body and mind is the starting point to understand what you need at any given time. Take a moment through the day and ask yourself "what do I need right now?" and wait for the answer. The first thing that pops into your head is usually exactly what you need in that moment. Your intuition is your best friend and it pays to listen to the nudges it gives you.

When I first arrived in the US it was after a very intense period of selling my home and packing up and preparing for the move, both personally and professionally. Then when I arrived it was straight into setting up from scratch again both personally and professionally. After about a month I noticed my demeanor change. Instead of connecting with people like I normally would by talking and saying hello to people in the lift, coffee shop etc. I would avoid eye contact. Because I had built up a habit of self-observation, I noticed this in myself and recognized that I had been running on empty. From my earlier experience of burnout, I put in place what works for me. I set the alarm earlier and mediated daily on waking and went to the gym before I started my day. Within days I noticed a change within myself and stuck to my daily regime to ensure I had the energy to get through. In fact, it was the days when I least felt like it that I knew I needed it the most. It was a daily decision made easier by knowing how much better I would feel.

Exercise

Think about your current energy levels and give yourself a score out of 10 for where you feel you are right now – 1 for I have no energy and can barely get out of bed to 10 I jump out of bed and have so much energy I need to find an outlet to burn it off. Where do you sit? Now that you have a number think about the different aspects I have covered such as mindfulness, doing something you love, scheduling time for yourself, microbreaks and exercise. Which of these areas are currently missing in your life or could be enhanced? How can you implement this? Write this down and at a minimum introduce at least one of these into your life starting today. Monitor how you feel in one week and if there is anything else on your list introduce this for one week whilst you continue to monitor how you feel. Continue this until you have established new habits to manage your energy and a new habit of observing and tapping into your intuition.

Chapter 17

Mental Resilience

Besides activity and skill what makes great salespeople great, is also their level of resilience. Resilience enables you to bounce back from setbacks and to stay on course towards your goals and objectives. Because of the nature of sales having mental resilience is an important factor that determines longer term success. There will be many setbacks and unforeseen challenges that will need to be navigated both from a practical standpoint and emotionally. How quickly and steadfastly you are able to do this will have a direct impact on your effectiveness as a salesperson and your overall success.

When I look at my younger sales self, I really was at the whim of my external environment – both good and bad. I hadn't yet developed my internal resilience and compass that could weather any storm. I had to be resilient from the inside out for the external influences not to cripple me at the knees as they sometimes did.

In 1990, Australia like most of the world had gone into recession. I was working at Yellow Pages which had an annual sales competition with an overseas trip. Two thirds the way through the sales year the results came out and I was in the top 10. In any other year I would have qualified for the trip but due to the severity of the recession my actual revenue hadn't met the minimum qualification for the trip.

At the time my sales manager was not engaged for personal reasons and was largely absent, however another sales manager from another team saw the results and gave me a pep talk. Because this sales manager had nothing to gain from my success, I really took onboard what she said and something inside me clicked. The next day I went to work with a different attitude and came in early and stayed late until I had reached my daily target that would get me on the trip – it was roughly equivalent to three times my actual target every single day for six weeks. This of course was not an easy feat so far into the year and when we were selling into "country" directories with much lower revenue. In fact, it had never been done before. The following morning, a senior manager who knew of my goal asked me if I had reached my target and I said yes. I saw the surprise in his eyes and I would tell myself it was just luck. But after three days in a row I knew it couldn't be just luck and that I was actually achieving this through my own efforts. With focused determination and a renewed confidence in my ability to hit the daily revenue target, I qualified and traveled to Hong Kong and Thailand at the end of the year.

However, my confidence and self-belief was only skin deep and I suffered from Imposter Syndrome. At the start of the trip each morning I would go to breakfast, and I was literally waiting for someone to say "you have not qualified" and send me back home. Sounds ridiculous now, but as a 20 year old it felt very real. I only relaxed when we got to Thailand after a week! The irony of this was the following year I was talking to a salesperson who realized who I was and said that their Manager was using my example of what was possible. At that point in my career I didn't believe in my abilities and needed someone else to believe in me, and even then, doubted if I was really good enough.

In 2001 I was back in New Zealand and had gone into IT recruitment. It was a baptism by fire, at the time I had never even used a computer and it was my first role after being away from the workforce for two years after having my daughter. I started well and I approached it like any other role – high activity and meet as many people as I could, and I was bringing in new sales. At the time there was a woman of a similar age to me who worked alongside me, who was very established and successful in her role. I found it difficult to work alongside her and my Manager at the time told me not to worry she was jealous of my early success.

Unfortunately, my Manager left the company and the role was taken up by this same woman. Life became unbearable as she targeted me for less than professional treatment. Because I hadn't developed the mental resilience and inner self belief her negativity towards me deeply affected me. Overnight I went from being a high achiever to having three consecutive months with no sales. She took this opportunity to fire me – a devastating blow as a single mother at the time and emotionally it crushed me.

I managed to find a new role and the weekend before I was due to start, I had what I would describe as a "mental episode." I returned to my home after being out for the day and immediately felt like someone was in my house. I rang my mum as I was so panicked, and she stayed on the phone as I walked through the house slowly opening every door and cupboard. I was so frightened I left my house and stayed the night at my mothers and couldn't sleep all night afraid of the dark and utterly convinced a murder was taking place that night at my own house. The following morning, I drove to my house and as I approached, I expected to see Police cars and yellow tape. To my astonishment there was nothing – just my lovely little, peaceful cottage on the waterfront. At that point I realized it was all in my head, but I couldn't work out why I had had such an episode. Talking to my sister about my experience she said "Rebecca you have the biggest fear of failure of anyone I know." I still had a lot of inner work to do.

Fast forward to 2018 and I was now in my late 40's and a recent empty nester, who had decided to move more than 6,000 miles to the land of opportunity in the US. I was excited to finally have some skin in the game. After making other people money and turning around their businesses, I could finally apply my sales ability in a company where I had ownership and would reap the rewards. This was my ticket!

However, we were green when it came to understanding the nuances of Hollywood and just how difficult it was going to be. I was new to the entertainment industry and until that point most of our business had been mainly New Zealand and Australian production companies with the odd exception. The board was also New Zealand based made up of men who had no background in Entertainment or knowledge of the industry in Hollywood with the exception of the CEO.

The expectation that I had, and the board too, was that it would take three months to get my first sale and gain quick traction from there. In fact, it took me five months to get my first small sale on a low budget production and in the first year I could count my sales on one hand. I could sense their impatience and lack of confidence in my ability, and in early 2019 I was told by my CEO I probably had three months at best before the board would look to replace me and send me packing back to New Zealand. Of course, this was devastating to hear. They hired someone with experience and connections in the entertainment industry but without significant sales experience or understanding of our technology, and then made me report to him which was tough to swallow. To add salt to the wound his demeanor changed significantly when he became my boss and I had to apply all of my experience in dealing with difficult customers to manage a difficult boss.

Had this happened to me 10 years prior it would have crippled me like before – it would have been my death knell. But because I had slowly built up my inner reserves through self-belief and mental resilience, I was able to persist despite the blow. The negative outside influence was no longer controlling me but rather I controlled it. I used the anger I felt at the situation and channeled it constructively into my work. And what also kept me motivated was I had invested in the company, excited by the technology and the opportunity and that part hadn't changed. I now believed in my ability at a much deeper level. I knew that if it was this difficult for me, it was going to be this difficult for anyone and I just had to persist. And persist I did.

The person they hired didn't bring in any sales and I was starting to see results. In the end he actually did me a favor. He showed that no amount of industry experience on its own could win a deal, it took persistent action and sales skill. He was fired and I kept going, making the calls and doing the demos. Over time we stopped being the industry newcomer and suddenly the studios were aware of us and we were being talked about. It took two years to get to the point where we were getting month on month sales revenue increase. This was by far the most challenging sales experience I had to date and the slowest.

If it were not for the resilience I had built up over many years, I wouldn't have survived this experience and probably would be back in New Zealand right now nursing my wounds. Thank goodness for adversity as it strengthens us. In every seemingly negative experience, there is a silver lining – a gift of learning from that experience. If you can take a growth mindset and look for the learning opportunity to get up again to face another day any setback won't be permanent. A failure is only permanent if you fail to get up again.

Exercise

Think about some of the major challenges you have had in your life. These can be both personal and professional. Write down what gifts you have received through these challenges. Write down everything that comes to mind. For example, for my latest challenge that I described, one of the gifts was it make me think about my future beyond the business I was in. If it had not been for that experience, I wouldn't have created new goals and may have landed with a thump after the business sold. In fact, I may not even have written these pages you are reading now if it were not for the board losing confidence in me and hiring a replacement, as I doubt I would have taken the actions that led me to this point.

Write down everything you can think of, especially if there is something that is causing you some mental distress currently. This exercise will get you to orient toward a growth mindset and see the gifts in adversity. Getting rid of the old mentality and seeing the experience in a new light can also open up new paths and opportunities.

Chapter 18

Working with Other People

Although sales can at times can feel like very solitary work, there are many situations where you will be interacting with other operational, presales teams or sales partners. These people can have a significant impact on the sales process and outcome, so it pays to work with them effectively. In the first chapter I talk about the qualities of being influential and these are also applicable to working well with other teams and/or people.

Having a high Emotional Quotient or EQ is the most important quality you can possess, to observe the emotional cues from the people you are working with and adapt to get the most out of them. Treat the people who can help you win the deal like they are a customer. If they can help or hinder, you need to be every bit as respectful and empathetic as you would if dealing with a client.

Rewarding people

I find rewarding people goes a long way in getting their buy-in and support. You want people to be just as invested as you are in the outcome and the best way to do this is to reward them accordingly. The reward can be both emotional and financial and the most effective is for it to be both. The law of reciprocity applies here. Whatever you do for them they will feel compelled to do for you and often they will do more. If you are not in a position to reward them financially through your company or who you work for look at other ways.

When I was in recruitment I worked closely with "resourcers" who would work with candidates whilst I was primarily working with the client that had the vacancy. The resourcers could be very helpful in knowing the pool of potential candidates for a role, however they didn't earn commission, but I did. The very first person I placed in a role came to me via a resourcer and my manager suggested I get a bottle of wine as a gift to say thank you for her efforts. It was the first time I had even thought of doing something like this before, especially out of my own pocket. However, it was the best thing I could have done. The resourcer was so appreciative of the gesture and it wasn't the last time she helped me find the right candidate. Since then I have always taken the opportunity to reward the people around me for work well done. Even small gestures like a coffee shout will go a long way.

Be quick to give credit

Even though you might close the deal, remember the people who helped get you to that point and be generous with your praise. And above all else be quick to give credit where it's due. People will remember this and be loyal. There's nothing worse than a self-congratulating salesperson on a win who forgets all the people who helped her get her there. You are not taking anything away from yourself or your achievement, you are lifting somebody else up who deserves to be recognized. Recognition is important to most people and can be a significant factor in people leaving their jobs – a lack of recognition. Recognize and give credit to those who help you and watch them support you over and over again.

People want to help

Interestingly they have found in research that people who ask for help in turn get more help. It seems that people intrinsically want to help others – human beings are hardwired to help, and it makes us feel good – it's a win/win. By asking people for help we are appealing to this part of their nature and in doing so we will build stronger connections and in turn they will be more willing to help in the future. It literally makes them feel good about themselves.

I remember when I was in my early 30's working in radio, an older colleague of mine made the observation that I often got help from people around me. She found this very interesting as it seemed to come easily to me, or so it seemed from her perspective. Looking back through the lens of someone now with more experience, I can see that this principle was at work. I was able to get help simply by asking. Of course, the *way* I asked was very important too. I asked in a way that showed that they had the expertise that was going to help me, and I was direct and specific. There was no manipulation or feeling on their part that they had to. It was always asked as a request with no expectation of fulfillment and I was always extremely thankful.

Appreciation

People will always do more when they feel appreciated and resentment can build when they feel they are not appreciated. Remember the last time you opened a door for a stranger, and they walked straight through without saying thank you, how did you feel? Probably a little annoyed if you're anything like me. But the opposite is true. If the person says thank you, we feel great and we want to do another good deed. That's what appreciation does it feeds both the giver and the recipient. The simple act of saying thank you will reward you tenfold. Next time someone in your team helps you, even if it's expected of them and part of their role, say thank you and sincerely. Be generous with your appreciation and you will find they will in turn be generous with their support.

Working with sales partners

In some businesses and sales roles, you are working with sales partners such as other distributors, dealers, resellers or retailers of your product or service. In this situation you need to collaborate together to become an effective sales channel. I personally have experienced both ends of the relationship – being the reseller selling third party software and being the software provider who is selling via a reseller. In the first experience where I was the reseller for third party software providers, the experience was varied depending on the company. At best it was collaborative and a true partnership. At worst it was like I was an employee to a very unappreciative sales manager. What I have found from this experience is that if you find yourself in the position of working with other companies who sell your product or service on your behalf, you want to support them as much as possible. Give them everything they need to sell your product or service as well as you would. Invest up front, build the relationship and set clear expectations early on how you will support them, how sales will be managed and reported, and build a close working relationship. Take the attitude that you are in service to them, not the other way around and this will create a solid foundation to work together.

Exercise

Have a day where you give a random act of kindness to your work colleagues. If you are working alone do this for a stranger. It could be anything from buying them a coffee to telling them something you appreciate about what they do for you, or putting money in a parking meter that has expired. Observe the affect it has on them and how it makes you feel. If you can make this a regular habit, see what impact it has both on the people you show kindness to and your own sense of wellbeing.

Chapter 19

Customer Service and Sales

Although it may seem obvious – that a good salesperson is also customer service oriented – this does not always hold true. In fact, it's one of the things that sets apart the mediocre from the exceptional – exceptional customer service. Every interaction you have with a client is showing them what it's like to do business with you and if they are an existing customer your level of customer service is telling them how much you appreciate their business. If they feel appreciated like the law of reciprocity, they will feel indebted to stay with you.

For some salespeople getting the deal is the end goal and what happens after is far less important. But just like a marriage this is when the hard work starts. And if you are wanting to build the customer into a long term strategic account it will take time, dedication and a commitment to customer service. As the salesperson you have the power to influence their perception and the likelihood that they will be a long term customer. I have had customers in my career that I have bent over backwards to make them happy, like the proverbial swan gliding on the water with feet paddling madly underneath. Some clients knew the effort I was going to and for some it wasn't visible, but what matters most is that they were impressed with our service.

The customer's perception is always right

You have probably heard the adage that "the customer is always right." A more accurate statement is their *perception* is always right. Whatever that perception may be, it's your responsibility to maintain it if it's positive or change it if it's not. Sometimes you might feel that their perception is not warranted, regardless their perception is real to them. Out in the marketplace they are talking, and your reputation and brand is dependent on that talk being positive. Let's take a look at what aspects help shift perceptions the most.

Do what you say you will do

The number one rule for customer service. There is nothing worse than saying you will do something and not delivering on that promise. I recall when I was selling radio advertising I had a potential new customer who was with a competitor and they asked for a proposal with a promotional element including a creative idea. I went to our head of promotions at the radio station and he was very slow in coming back with any tangible ideas that I could include in a proposal. It got to the point where I felt it was too late to go back – too much time had passed, so I didn't go back and thought that this is an opportunity that I will have to let pass. About six months later I was at a networking function and this person was there. I felt so embarrassed it was obvious from the look on his face he was unimpressed. It was an important lesson for me. No matter what follow-through. I could have put more pressure on the internal person that I was waiting on to deliver what I needed – and kept the client in the loop so he knew there was a delay, but it was coming. There is no exception to this rule – always do what you say you will do.

Creative problem solving

Sometimes things don't go as smoothly as planned and you may have a problem that takes some thought and teamwork to find a solution. A client doesn't want to know as much about the problem as they do about the solution. Some people go to pains to explain why they are experiencing a problem, and this can sometimes make things worse as it's not putting the client in the front and center. Put yourself in their shoes and think about what you would like to hear. My guess is you want a brief description of the problem but more importantly what you are going to do to solve it and by when.

When it comes to customer service and sales you are representing the interests of the customer within your company and managing the internal process so that the customer is happy and hopefully impressed. A good salesperson will show leadership in managing expectations on both sides and initiative in finding a solution. Take responsibility for the customer's perception and you will find yourself doing what it takes to keep them a happy and satisfied customer.

Sometimes you have to take it on the chin and smile

There will be times when a customer is not happy and you will have to deal with the situation the best way you can. It would be impossible to have 100% of customers impressed 100% of the time. If the customer gets emotional this is the one time when you *don't* want to mirror. Stay calm and remain focused on a solution and keep your tone and language focused squarely on the customer and their perspective, whilst gently bringing them to a productive solution focused conversation.

I recall when I was working for a Mom & Pop graphic design and website development business and a customer contacted me whilst the owners were on holiday in Fiji. This customer was a well-known chef and expected quick responses to support requests for her website – as she rightly should. However, on this occasion there was little I was able to do other than give her the owner's contact details in Fiji as she requested. She was yelling at me down the phone and I just had to suck it up, be polite and do whatever I could do to help the situation. Remember in these situations you are getting people at their worst not their best so try to put it in that context. If you keep your composure, you're more likely to recover the situation and the customer.

How to diffuse a situation

There are ways to diffuse a situation before it escalates. The easiest way to do this is go into solution mode as quickly as you can. Most people get agitated when they fear they are not going to get what they need and the moment they realize they will, they become a lot calmer. In my early 20's I worked for an Australian airline, Ansett, doing out-bound sales calls to businesses to convert them from the major competitor Qantas and maintain existing customers. This was also around the time the Frequent Flyer program was launched and the airline was inundated with calls and we had to help. I recall getting an agitated customer who had been on hold and spoken to many different people but still couldn't get access to the airport lounge as a new airline lounge member. I said to him in a very calm and comforting tone "don't worry I'll take care of this and make sure you will get into the lounge today." That's all I needed to do to calm him down. On all the other calls the people were trying to understand the problem and why his access was being denied rather than resolving the immediate problem of lounge access that day, which was causing him to become more agitated. I immediately arranged a temporary pass so he could access the lounge straight away and then dealt with the cause as a secondary matter. On the call he asked to speak to my manager and I thought I was in trouble. In fact, he wanted to praise me. Making someone feel like you are going to solve their problem and be personally responsible in doing so, will not only deescalate but will also win you legions of fans.

Setting expectations

Setting the right expectations will also set you up for a better outcome and a more satisfied customer. It also pays to do this early in the process to avoid any negative perceptions or disappointment from having to reset customer expectations. This is where under promising and over delivering really works in your favor. Remember to set expectations through the entire supply chain so that it all goes as smoothly as possible.

The end doesn't justify the means

How you get a sale is just as important as getting the sale. It's your brand perception that's at stake through the customer's experience of the sale process. Getting a sale at all costs can sometimes be too costly. I remember doing a personality test when I was about 21 when I was working for Yellow Pages as part of their personal development program and this was identified as something about me – I overused this justification. Today I operate quite differently, but I do recall this test quite clearly and even as a 21 year old it was food for thought. Only two years earlier I had won a competition selling small appliances where I won a travel prize based on selling the highest revenue of a particular brand. I had been extremely motivated and was the lead salesperson by a large margin. One particular sale came to mind as the customer wanted a food processor as a gift for his wife. I sold him on the benefits of the food processor that was the brand in the competition, despite knowing it was probably the most inferior product amongst the brands we sold. He came back days later very disappointed, but I did not offer a refund or exchange which was within my power to do so. I was more concerned with winning the competition than offering the best possible customer service. The end never justifies the means – I hate to think the perception this customer had of myself, the company I worked for and the brand I sold to him. Thankfully with maturity I changed and thankfully for all of us our personalities, attitudes and abilities are not set in stone and we are far more malleable than we realize.

Exercise

Think about your current role and the interactions you have with customers. How can you inject a more customer centric approach to what you do? Are there any areas in your sales process that don't give the best customer experience and how can you change that?

Chapter 20

Selling from a Woman's Perspective

Sales on the whole tends to attract more men than women, with some industries having a higher representation of women such as advertising sales and some with more men such as IT sales. I'm not sure why this is but it does mean there are some considerations when selling as a woman. And now more than ever with women entrepreneurship on the rise more and more women will be finding themselves making pitches and selling, and sometimes to other women.

As a young woman I very much wanted to be treated as an equal and to have professional business conversations. I was very careful with how I dressed so that the conversation would be focused squarely on the business at hand and not on my attire. In my early career my customer was more likely to be a man and I felt extremely uncomfortable with anything other than direct eye contact, so was careful with my dress code and body language. This is where setting boundaries is important and showing what is acceptable and what is not. I recall when I was in radio advertising and I took over a customer account who was a car mechanic. This was of course a very masculine environment and the owner spoke to me in a very flirtatious way. I didn't appreciate this and did not engage with him in that way and kept it strictly professional. I could tell by the way he was talking my predecessor also a woman, had entertained his flirtatious behavior to maintain him as a customer. As a result, I didn't get any repeat business, but it was not the type of business I wanted nor needed to achieve results. However, during that time I still hadn't learnt to set boundaries as strongly as I needed to or to say no. On another occasion I had a potential customer come into the Radio Station to discuss advertising for a new business venture. My intuition raised two flags – that something wasn't right about the business with not enough capital for any significant advertising, and that he seemed too interested in me. After our meeting I put together a proposal and when I rang to set a time to present, he gave me his home address. Because of my earlier intuitive feeling about him and the business, I should have at that point said no I can't come out but can meet in the city or at the Radio Station. But instead I drove out and happened to have a car accident on the way and when I rang him to say I couldn't make it he was extremely apologetic, and I never heard from him again. Today this would never happen to me as I have learnt to qualify opportunities and set boundaries, so that I sell and do business on my terms and I am quite prepared to walk away if it's not.

Over the years the number of women in decision-making and executive roles has drastically increased and I do find a sort of kinship when dealing with women in business. They have had the same struggles as me and I think as women we enjoy working together especially in male dominated professions. I see being a woman in sales as an asset, especially as gender equality continues to increase in the workplace and there are more women executives. On the flip side being a woman in sales I can often be underestimated, and when it comes to sales that can actually be a **good** thing. You know the sports team that is the underdog that nobody rates and because of that they can surprise their opposition and overwhelm them. Being underestimated in sales is not too different – people have their guard down. And when they have their guard down it usually means you get a lot more information and you can drive the sale forward in a way that is a lot harder to achieve if they have their guard up, which may be the case with a male equivalent.

Looking back at my sales career the situation for women has definitely improved, however there is still some unconscious bias – and sometimes conscious bias towards women. The area where this is most keenly felt is in what I would call the "boys' network." The relationships built on the golf course or over a drink after work where women are more likely to be excluded. The informal nature of these makes it more difficult for women to break into the inner circle. If I was to search for a silver lining in the current pandemic it would be that this disadvantage for women will dissipate somewhat – at least for the time that social distancing remains in place. And by the time this period is over our habits will have changed, hopefully resulting in more inclusion for women. Time will tell. Until then, now is a great time to build strong relationships. As a woman in sales you stand out which is a good thing. In sales you want to be memorable.

Exercise

What I have found to be very useful is women's networks where you can find camaraderie and support. There are many industry/women specific networks that you can find through a simple google search or ask people you know in your industry what networks they belong to. You will find by joining it will give you access to like-minded female professionals and mentors and coaches that can help you on your personal and professional journey. Right now is a great time as there is no geographical limitation with video conferencing being the accepted norm, so no matter your situation or time constraints it's much easier to take advantage of these networking organizations. You might also discover potential new leads as well.

Chapter 21

Sales Strategy

What I have outlined in the sales process is taking a micro view of how to approach an opportunity from the initial approach through to closing the deal. The macro view of sales would be the sales strategy and overall approach to both Business Development and Account/Relationship Management. If you are primarily responsible for the sales function in your business this will be something that you will need to be across. And even if you're not, it's good to understand this so that when you are making decisions as to where to prioritize your time and sales effort, it aligns with the overall strategy. Let's take a look at what a sales strategy might cover.

Your Market

What is your market in terms of overall size and where do you sit in it? Are there distinct vertical markets and do you have geographical markets? Do you have unexplored opportunities within your market such as channel partners or a new offering that will unlock a new market? Where do you see the market heading and where do you need to adapt to either remain relevant or to capitalize on opportunities?

Your primary focus – the ideal customer

Where do you make the most money the most easily? This is your sweet spot and where you need to focus your sales efforts. Identify the type of customers that make the most revenue for you – the 80/20 rule – 20 percent of your customers will make 80 percent of the revenue. Who are they and do they fall into a specific part of the market?

Who are you selling to?

Identify the roles of the influencers and decision-makers. Generally, they will fall into groups for example executive level decision-makers and operational influencers. Sometimes depending on the industry, the influencers and decision-makers can have a more specific role e.g. CFO for decisionmaker and IT Manager for influencer. Understand the different roles as this will feed into your marketing strategy.

Your Competitors

Who are your major competitors? What part of the market is each competitor strong in and what are the threats they present? Where do you see them growing and where do you see them diminishing? What opportunities does this present to you?

Your strengths and weaknesses

What are your strengths and weaknesses in relation to your competition and to what the market needs right now and are anticipated in the future?

Your Positioning

Based on your understanding of the market, your competitors and your strengths and weaknesses, what is the best way to position yourself in the market? What is your strongest USP? How do you think you should approach the market with this USP? – this will feed into your marketing strategy.

Pricing

How does your pricing compare with your competitors? Can you use pricing to drive more customers into the more profitable parts of your business? How can you simplify pricing if it's complex? Has your pricing evolved with your business? How does your pricing support your strategy? E.g. exclusivity to attract a high margin, high quality customer or a lower price to drive more sales and higher brand exposure to create a bigger footprint in the market.

Goals and objectives

What is your sales goals for the coming financial year and where do you want to see your revenue and margins? How does this translate into sales targets for yourself or your sales team? Do you have an overall number you want to achieve or do you want to break this down into objectives within categories?

Action Plan

Create a clear action plan based on the sales strategy and the goals and objectives you want to achieve and a completion date for each action.

A sales strategy is never static and will evolve over time as the business develops and the market changes. If you are managing a sales team the sales strategy is a great way to guide the team and make sure they are focusing on the priorities for the business. And at the other end of the scale if you are a one person business a sales strategy will help cement your sales direction.

Exercise

If you don't already have one, develop a sales strategy that sets the direction for your sales function within your business. If you do, review it and made sure it's current and actionable. A strategy is only as good as its execution.

Chapter 22

Sales Tools

For a lot of salespeople administration duties is not something they enjoy doing and can be relegated to the bottom of the priority list. In my career I have generally been a bit of a stickler for keeping accurate records and having the right information at my fingertips. The driving force behind this has not been any need for order or structure, but rather having the right information at the right time helps me to sell more effectively and be more efficient.

In the modern economy data is even more crucial and it's only as valuable as it is accurate. When I first started out in sales everything was manual and having a computer at your desk was unheard of. I wrote notes for all of my interactions and had a "card" for every client or opportunity. My memory was never going to be enough and I needed the notes to recall the conversation and understand what action was required next. I also used a day planner religiously. Any next step or action would be written in my planner on the day it was needed to be done by. And if there were multiple steps each one would be in a day in my planner as an actionable item. If I didn't get to it that day, I would move it to another day. That was how I prioritized and managed the input of sales data through the sales pipeline. Now we have multiple software tools and applications that can make this process much easier, but the principle of accurate data, notes and actions still apply.

Customer Relationship Management (CRM) system

Probably the most important tool for sales is the Customer Relationship Management system or CRM. Instead of the "cards" I used we now have software or a CRM that can manage the sales process digitally. The CRM can also manage the overall "relationship" with the client providing a central source of information for any sales and customer information. There are a number of CRM's on the market and the size of your business will partly determine which one is best suited to your needs. But having the software is one thing and using it is another. I've highlighted below the key areas where a CRM can help the sales process and the best way to use it to your advantage.

Leads

Leads are company or individual names that have yet to be approached but are potential opportunities. These could be business cards collected at a networking event, companies you notice while driving and scribble down the name, companies you have researched online, people you have found or connected with on LinkedIn or suggestions from other clients or people you know. You will need a digital repository for all of the names you collect. This will be the starting point for development of your "sales pipe."

Opportunities

After you make contact with a lead and you have started the sales process you will convert it from a lead to an opportunity. This just means that you have enough information to qualify it as a potential opportunity. Most CRMS will allow you to set the "stage" of the opportunity. For example, you could set each stage as meeting, discovery, evaluation, proposal, negotiation and then a final step to close as won or lost. Again, it's totally dependent on the industry you are in as to what stages you should have, but this is a very typical example. The idea behind it is you can show the progression of the opportunity generally tied to milestones. For example, if you have set the first meeting the opportunity would be at "meeting." Subsequent meetings would be at "discovery" customer testing of your services or product would be at "evaluation", when you send a proposal it would be at "proposal" and when you send an Agreement for signing this would be at "negotiation." Most CRMS will allow you to tailor these stages to reflect your sales process.

Financial Forecasting

Having accurate records in CRM will also help with forecasting. As I've described above having opportunities that are at stages and tied to milestones can be used to input into a forecast. How you apply the data to the forecast is up to each individual business but it's a good starting point and can be refined depending on how accurate the forecasts are.

Relationship management

CRM's are also helpful to have a central source of truth for all sales information relating to a client. This is especially helpful if there are multiple touchpoints across your business, say for example customer service or support who are also having customer interactions. If someone in your business is having a conversation with your client, from a sales perspective and overall relationship management you want to be across that. Everyone has had an experience when you feel like the left hand doesn't know what the right hand is doing when dealing with a company. Having a CRM that notes all customer interactions will avoid that and provide a much better customer experience. It also gives greater visibility of a customer's interaction with your company and be helpful to track any new opportunities.

Sales activity management

CRM is a great way to manage sales activity. Unlike in my early days in sales, you no longer need to keep a daily planner to note any action required with a particular client or opportunity. But like any software it's only as valuable as it's being utilized. This is where there needs to be a discipline to keep on top of it.

For me I just transferred a methodical paper based system to an electronic one. I use the CRM as a reminder of any action that's required for opportunities, every day I look at the opportunity pipe and look at each opportunity to make sure there is nothing there that doesn't require any action OR could benefit from an action e.g. a new development that I think will interest a particular client. Looking at CRM every day will make sure you stay across everything and nothing falls through the cracks. Because I see it this way, it seems less like administration and more like making sure my opportunity pipeline is primed.

Sales Reporting

This is most beneficial for someone managing a team or the sales function in a business, providing accurate forecasting via sales reporting in the CRM. However, from a personal perspective you can look at the win/losses and understand what your win ratio is – the number of opportunities you have won against the number lost. It can also give insight into how long it is taking you on average to close a sale and what areas you are having the most success. You will probably have a feel on this already but seeing the stats from sales reporting can provide further insights and less subjectivity. It's just another tool for self-improvement giving you something else to measure yourself against for continual improvement. Try not to beat yourself up if the stats don't look good, use it as a motivating tool to improve over time. And if they are great there is always room for improvement!

Software integration

Some CRM's can provide integration with other software applications for example email, phone & campaign management giving a centralized space for salespeople to do their work without having to hop in and out of applications. These integrations also make it much easier to track client communications in one centralized area.

Marketing

Having an up to date database with accurate data feeds into the marketing strategy which will hopefully generate leads to feed into the sales pipeline. Although marketing is a separate discipline, the ultimate goal of marketing is to generate sales whether that be through brand awareness or direct call to action for lead generation. Keeping information in CRM up to date will ultimately help yourself.

Exercise

Review how you are currently using CRM and see if there are any areas that you can improve to support your sales process. This can be at an individual or team level. Write down the areas that you feel are not working as well as they could and what steps you need to take to improve – for example reviewing your current CRM, reviewing the stages, data accuracy or more detailed updates and what they should include. Write an action plan for the changes.

Chapter 23

Hiring & Managing a Sales Team

Being responsible to bring in sales and being responsible for the *people* that bring in sales is a very different skill set. Often a sales manager will come from a sales background – typically a first time sales manager will be hired from a sales team, as I was. Or you could be a business owner without any sales experience hiring and managing salespeople.

My one and only experience of sales management was a baptism by fire. I was working for a software development company and had been with the company for five years. During my time there I had bought on a number of large accounts and as a result the company had undergone significant growth and there was an opportunity to expand the sales team and for myself to lead it, so I was excited at the opportunity.

It was a steep learning curve and the second time I was to come close to burn out. I put very high expectations on myself and definitely didn't follow the "Managing Energy" tips in this book. The concept of microbreaks was to come after this experience and with the drive to succeed I let go of some of the good habits I had developed such as meditation and separation of work and homelife.

Hiring salespeople

Although I didn't get any specific sales management training, thankfully I had done recruitment, so I at least understood the basics of interviewing and managing the recruitment process. And being a salesperson myself I knew what questions to ask to uncover the traits of a person. However, one mistake I made on more than one occasion was to not to listen to my instincts when interviewing someone. For every bad hire I have made, there has always been a moment when I would get an answer that raises a flag with me in a gut instinct way. Sometimes it can seem minor in the overall interview, so from a logical point of view it seems too insignificant to make a decision not to hire from that one concern. But without fail, every single time this has happened the concern that was flagged by my gut instinct turned out to be true. The cost of hiring someone who is not right for the role, far outweighs the cost of waiting for the right person.

It's best to start with very high-level questions to make the person feel very comfortable with you. Also, keep in mind that you are selling the role to them as much as they are selling themselves to you. But gradually as you see they are comfortable ask tougher and tougher questions. A good salesperson should be able to think on their feet so it's OK to put them through their paces. You really want to understand how they will be in a sales situation. Ask them about their achievements and make sure they are specific and also drill down on how they were involved – and did they drive the process. You really want to understand how involved they were and what parts of the sales process they were responsible for – some people will describe an achievement that was team based and you want to uncover that. You also want to understand if they are comfortable chasing new business or prefer to strengthen and build existing relationships and factor that into what your business needs. You will discover this by asking specific questions about their experience *and* what they enjoy doing. I also find it helpful to ask about their interests outside of work as this will give you a lot of insight into their character. Other aspects you want to understand about them is their work ethic – salespeople are largely working independently so you want them to have a solid work ethic in order to be self-motivated. What motivates them? Some salespeople will be motivated by money and that's OK – as long as your role caters for that in a commission or bonus incentive plan. Some people are looking to grow their sales career or are motivated by achievements, it's good to know what drives them. This will also weed out those that aren't driven – it's unlikely they will be a high performing salesperson without high levels of motivation.

Managing to a salesperson's strengths

What you'll find in salespeople is that they will typically fall into three categories. The first is the business development salesperson who enjoys the "chase" and closing the deal but will get bored with the details after the sale is closed and frustrated with the details and customer service required to manage an account long term.

The second is the salesperson who is a "relationship" person who derives job and personal satisfaction from developing strong customer relationships and delivering service to their customers. This is how they sell – through relationships.

The third salesperson is a combination of both. They are an allrounder in that they can do both business development and relationship management. What you will find is that their effectiveness at Business Development comes from their ability to build relationships, but they also enjoy the thrill of winning new business. However, they will have a sense of ownership once the business is won and will apply a business development mentality to account management to grow the account.

From reading these three descriptions you will probably agree that the third seems the most desirable. However, it's unlikely that you will have a team made up with just this one type of salesperson, and sometimes you won't have one at all – they are a rare breed. So, it will be important to play to their strengths so that the sales role, targets and expectations are in line with their sales style. A relationship builder will find it difficult to pick up the phone and make cold calls, but if given an account that's had a previous bad experience will be more committed to turning it around through building strong relationships. Whilst the excitement chasing a win will propel the Business Development salesperson to pick up the phone, and much less likely to enjoy the commitment required to turn around an account.

For some teams splitting the roles will make sense and having a handover from business development to relationship management once the sale is closed. If this does not fit the industry standard, you will either have to have allowances in how you allocate accounts to suit the style of the salesperson, or provide training to help upskill in the area that doesn't come naturally to them. However, I have found that most salespeople will naturally fall on a spectrum between business development and relationship/account management and the more you align their roles to their natural preference, the better the results.

Incentives

Most salespeople will perform better if given an incentive. In fact, that is what attracted me to sales in the first place and for a large part of my career was my sole motivation. I even remember turning down a role as a travel agent when I was 18 when I discovered it wasn't commission based – even though there would have been a huge amount of free or discounted travel and as a travel lover I would have been amazing in the role. Without the financial incentive I just wasn't interested. And you'll find most salespeople are the same.

Incentives can also drive sales behavior so depending on the business objectives you can tweak incentives to drive sales in a certain area. This can be quite effective, however there can also be a downside that you need to consider. When faced with the choice of selling what will make money or selling what is best for the customer, often money will win over the customer. This is not only in the best interest of the customer but not in the best interest of your business in the longer term. I have seen incentive plans backfire because of this. I worked for a company that switched to this model and a software product was sold before the customer was ready. When the renewal came up the customer had only had six months use instead of 12 and was very unhappy that they had to renew. This was the "handover" scenario I described earlier so the original salesperson had little incentive to delay the initial sale to suit the customers timing and was out of the picture by the time the renewal came around. There is always a balance between driving sales behavior and keeping the interest of the customer at the center.

The other extreme is when I was working in radio and was on commission only. The company used the "stick" as well the carrot in that they deducted any commission that was paid where the customer had not paid their invoice inside 90 days. This happened on one occasion to me and it hurt so much as a single working mother I never let it happen again. One time I had a customer that was nearing 90 days with an unpaid invoice and I ended up walking with him to the bank to get the money to avoid the commission deduction! It was effective in driving sales behavior but ultimately, I'm not sure it gave the best customer experience or sent the right message to the salespeople that they were valued and supported.

For some salespeople the desire to achieve and win is what matters most. In this case recognition of their efforts and achievements can be highly motivating. Having a "leader's board" or an award that recognizes their achievements can motivate both them and the rest of the sales team. In chapter 11 I shared with you my story of winning the New Zealand Defence Force account which took me two years, by which time I had moved into a sales management role and no longer incentivized for individual account wins but rather the overall team result. Even though I wasn't financially recognized for the sale, I was so excited by the enormous win I couldn't sleep at all that night. At that stage I had been in sales for over 25 years so was surprised at my own reaction. It proved to me that even though I had started out in sales because of the financial incentives, the reason I stayed in sales for so long was the satisfaction and adrenalin rush of a win.

For good salespeople this is what will drive them and as their leader it's up to you to support them in any way you can so that they can excel. Remove any barriers, give them the tools they need, be attentive to their needs whilst giving them space to do their job and you have a recipe for sales success.

Dealing with non-performance

If you are like me, you may discover that the gut feeling you had about someone but ignored and subsequently hired, has come to pass. From my personal experience it's best dealt with quickly and as considerately as possible. For some people you may be able to restructure their role to suit their strengths, for example they have a technical bent and can be utilized in a presales role to support the sales team or a reallocation of accounts that may fit them better. But in some instances, that's not an option and having a poor performing salesperson can affect overall morale as there is the perception that poor performance is tolerated.

Having strong expectations and clear targets will assist in weeding out non-performance as it will be apparent very quickly if they are missing the mark. But sometimes it can take people time to get to grips with the role and it's important that if they show a willing attitude to learn and grow, a good work ethic and some natural sales aptitude that you invest this time to let them come up to speed and grow into the role. It's equally important to show that you are willing to support your team. It's a fine balance between setting expectations and measuring to these, whilst supporting them in the process.

Chapter 24

Sales in 2020 and Beyond

The global pandemic we are currently in presents unique challenges but also immense opportunity. It's not about how to survive but rather how to flourish during this time. It is a time to dig deep and search for the opportunities that exist amidst a time of great change. Some aspects of how we do business will most likely change permanently and those who adapt quickly will reap the rewards. The days of meeting in person are over for the foreseeable future, and business development will be much tougher and likely take longer. However for those that persist it's still possible to win new customers in this environment. Where relationships have been established it will be much easier to continue to generate sales albeit over phone and video conference calls. For companies that are just entering the market at this time, the sales and marketing strategy will need to be revisited to take into account social distancing in sales. This is a time to reap the hard work done in the last few years to get through to a time when a vaccine will make face to face meetings the norm again. Until then, salespeople are becoming adept at video calls and emails with a compelling subject line to entice an existing or new customer.

For the business I am in it will only accelerate our growth in the US and globally, with our USP facilitating remote production. Pre-Covid this was to drive efficiencies. Post-Covid our technology will enable social distancing. Personally, I am expecting great things.

I hope that whatever business you are in you can use the tips and tools within these pages to position yourself to flourish in these times. Some of the strongest businesses were started during a recession. There has never been a better time to lead with innovation and to take a creative approach to problem solving – right now the world needs it.

It has been a rewarding experience for me personally putting 30+ years of sales experience on paper. My greatest wish is that these pages help you to shape your sales future and inspire you to be your best sales self.

BUSINESS
BOOKS

Business Books

Business Books publishes practical guides
and insightful non-fiction for beginners and professionals.
Covering aspects from management skills, leadership and
organizational change to positive work environments, career
coaching and self-care for managers, our books are a valuable
addition to those working in the world of business.

15 Ways to Own Your Future
Take Control of Your Destiny in Business and in Life
Michael Khouri
A 15-point blueprint for creating better collaboration, enjoyment, and success in business and in life.
Paperback: 978-1-78535-300-0 ebook: 978-1-78535-301-7

The Common Excuses of the Comfortable Compromiser
Understanding Why People Oppose Your Great Idea
Matt Crossman
Comfortable compromisers block the way of anyone trying to change anything. This is your guide to their common excuses.
Paperback: 978-1-78099-595-3 ebook: 978-1-78099-596-0

The Failing Logic of Money
Duane Mullin
Money is wasteful and cruel, causes war, crime and dysfunctional feudalism. Humankind needs happiness, peace and abundance. So banish money and use technology and knowledge to rid the world of war, crime and poverty.
Paperback: 978-1-84694-259-4 ebook: 978-1-84694-888-6

Mastering the Mommy Track
Juggling Career and Kids in Uncertain Times
Erin Flynn Jay
Mastering the Mommy Track tells the stories of everyday working mothers, the challenges they have faced, and lessons learned.
Paperback: 978-1-78099-123-8 ebook: 978-1-78099-124-5

Modern Day Selling
Unlocking Your Hidden Potential
Brian Barfield
Learn how to reconnect sales associates with customers and unlock hidden sales potential.
Paperback: 978-1-78099-457-4 ebook: 978-1-78099-458-1

The Most Creative, Escape the Ordinary, Excel at Public Speaking Book Ever
All The Help You Will Ever Need in Giving a Speech
Philip Theibert
The 'everything you need to give an outstanding speech' book, complete with original material written by a professional speech-writer.
Paperback: 978-1-78099-672-1 ebook: 978-1-78099-673-8

On Business And For Pleasure
A Self-Study Workbook for Advanced Business English
Michael Berman
This workbook includes enjoyable challenges and has been de-signed to help students with the English they need for work.
Paperback: 978-1-84694-304-1

Small Change, Big Deal
Money as if People Mattered
Jennifer Kavanagh
Money is about relationships: between individuals and between communities. Small is still beautiful, as peer lending model, micro-credit, shows.
Paperback: 978-1-78099-313-3 ebook: 978-1-78099-314-0

Readers of ebooks can buy or view any of these bestsellers by clicking on the live link in the title. Most titles are published in paperback and as an ebook. Paperbacks are available in traditional bookshops. Both print and ebook formats areavailable online.

Find more titles and sign up to our readers' newsletter at http://www.jhpbusiness-books.com/

Facebook: https://www.facebook.com/JHPNonFiction/

Twitter: @JHPNonFiction